The Transformation
Case Studies

Bertrand Jouslin de Noray
Elisabeth Ballery
Shoji Shiba
David Walden

Transformation Case Studies

Bertrand Jouslin de Noray, Author
Elisabeth Ballery, Author
Shoji Shiba, Author
David Walden, Author

Daniel Picard, Project Leader
Michele Kierstead, Production
Janet MacCausland, Graphic Design

GOAL/QPC

12B Manor Parkway, Salem, NH 03079-2862
Phone: 800.643.4316 or 603.893.1944
Fax: 603.870.9122
service@goalqpc.com
www.goalqpc.com

Printed in the United States of America

First Edition
10 9 8 7 6 5 4 3 2 1

ISBN 1-57681-081-X

Preface

It is a pleasure to launch this third in a series of three books on transformation. In the first book, *The Transformation Desktop Guide*, the reader is introduced to the basics of a transformation system as practiced by some of the best-run organizations in the world. In the second book, *The Transformation Fieldbook*, the authors, Stephen Hacker and Bertrand Jouslin de Noray, present coaching and guidance on implementing the key points of transformation. Section 1 of this third book, *Transformation Case Studies*, provides examples of transformation in organizations from Europe, Asia, and the United States. In section 2 of this book Shoji Shiba of Japan and David Walden of CQM provide interpretation of what these cases mean in the development of new approaches to breakthrough management.

GOAL/QPC has been a leader for over two decades in discovering and developing the leading edge of quality and making it available to everyone. We have believed for some time now that the human dimension has been underserved in quality improvement. It is our hope that this trilogy on transformation will significantly improve the people dimension of an organization's improvement efforts. And finally, we believe this trilogy is an exciting addition to GOAL/QPC's growing suites of products on facilitation, teams, performance management, and project management. Visit us a **www.goalqpc.com** to learn more about these products.

Bob King
Founder and CEO, GOAL/QPC

Foreword

Transformation. What a fitting topic for EOQ to explore as it celebrates its 50th anniversary. No doubt, in 1956 the ideas of control and, later, improvement were topics of transformation.

In the last 50 years the world has transformed, and while the tools of control and improvement still offer organizations breathtaking opportunity, they alone are not enough. With product life cycles of less than a year; with nanotechnology and biotechnology just beginning to impact our lives; with global (Internet-enabled) markets; with a warming, resource-limited planet; and with turbulent world politics—new tools are needed.

We must discover, maybe even invent, new tools, so I applaud this groundbreaking, visionary work of the EOQ and Bertrand Jouslin de Noray (EOQ's Secretary General.) Visionaries invite us to change, explore, question, and grow, yet it is human nature to resist change. But change we must if we are to flourish in our rapidly changing world.

It is certain, too, that new tools, without new ways of collaborating in the use of these tools, will leave us wanting. The failures of quality are seldom failures of the tools. The tools cannot fail, but we struggle for adequate ways to use them in our complex world. EOQ's rich, diverse culture is a wonderful laboratory for learning new ways to work together, in EOQ "Camps" and in their use of "The World Café."

While we join EOQ in celebrating its first 50 years, the world waits expectantly for the fruits of this work. Congratulations EOQ and thank you for leading! ASQ and the rest of the world quality community look forward to working with you to fulfill Dr. Juran's vision, making the 21st century the century of quality!

Paul E. Borawski, CAE
Executive Director and Chief Strategic Officer, ASQ

Contents

A Note to You

This publication is the result of a common effort of organizations and individuals, working together over many years to help organizations find new ways of leading and reaching their essentials. We would like to mention the network of Summer Camps gathering 300 participants from 30 countries, EOQ, ESQH, TPC, GOAL/QPC, ASQ, and many others that we cannot name here. They have all made contributions of their experiences and skills.

This book represents research efforts made by different centers to better understand transformation in organizations. It is in direct connection with two books published by GOAL/QPC, namely *The Transformation Desktop Guide* and *The Transformation Fieldbook*.

The Transformation Desktop Guide calls upon new mindsets to achieve transformational results. The text invites you to consider the essentials of self and the organization. It gives you practical ways to start and sustain the journey—a long journey requiring clear intention and energy. Finally, it speaks to the spirit of creation, which makes the route to transformation a rewarding experience.

The Transformation Fieldbook brings you diverse concepts, methods, and practices to accomplish transformational change. It is in a format that allows you to choose what tools or techniques are a best fit for your situation. The end target is to help you in reaching your essentials, thus moving the organization forward in step-function improvement.

We invite the reader to refer to these sister texts. The book you have opened targets examples of organizations that have successfully implemented transformation for a long period of time.

This book is linked with the research made by Shoji Shiba on transformation in organizations. Two books detail the present results of his research. The first is the translation to French of his book, *Breakthrough Management*, which was written in Japanese and was awarded the 2004 Nikkei Quality Control Literature Award by the Deming Committee; the second book is a rewrite in English of this prize-winning Japanese book, with new content added.

Why we launched this research

For almost 20 years, we have felt that Western management methods no longer fit with the economic globalization. Indeed, how can we stay competitive against Asian companies who are able to manufacture high quality products while paying salaries that are ten times less than those of the West? The gap is too vast to be breached by a reduction of the workforce, an improvement of productivity, or mergers and acquisitions. Relocation isn't a long-range solution either, because it restricts the creation of knowledge and experience to these new countries and locations, meaning that, ultimately, economic power will swing to their side (which is already happening in certain fields of activity).

Other ways need to be found

The situation, if you step back to consider it, is not unprecedented. Companies have experienced deep changes before that were, in the end, necessary for their own survival. The emergence of mass production in the twenties and the raising of oil prices in the sixties and seventies carried transformations along. The importance of the changes we face today is of the same type.

If we look back over past decades, the concepts, methods, and techniques proposed by the quality movement have been successful and widely used in the economy, allowing big improvements. But they are not enough to meet the present challenges of the fast-moving global economy. New ways have to be found, integrating breakthroughs, transformation, and innovation, that will lead to new paradigms.

Concerning this crisis, we can't help but be surprised by the unique thought that rules companies' management. The single principle they obey is: "Without a desperate race to growth and short-range profit, we're lost." But this leads to an absurd situation: only short-range gain is likely to reassure shareholders on long-term success! In the same way, the company is considered as a complex yet easy-to-dominate mechanism, as long as you have the right engineer to master the situation. Going against this single thought is considered heretical. It is a precept that remains true inside all management schools, business sectors, and more and more within the political world.

This situation seems excessive and dangerous, because it prevents companies from the possibility of turning toward solutions or initiatives that would be outside of this mold. Thus, very few listed companies dare to diverge, even slightly, from the narrow way that has been assigned. Yet, we sense that other ways exist, and we wish to discover them.

When we did our interviews, we were surprised to find a few isolated cases of successful companies that didn't apply the usual criteria. Financial matters weren't their ultimate goal, and yet, they proved to be even better performers than their competitors. Are they the only ones? Is there something to be learned through their example?

Suspicion and trust

We have been surprised to observe that the most shared behavior in organizations is suspicion. We wanted to meet with those where trust is the common value and see the effects on the efficiency of the organization. We have discovered that intention is a behavior present in companies experiencing breakthroughs, which leads them to outstanding results. We wanted to understand more in detail the effects of those behaviors on the organizations we studied.

Reaching the essentials

In the past, employees spent their whole work life in the same company or changed only a few times from one organization to another. But the rapid change in the economy has introduced flexibility and diversity into the work life of an employee. Is it possible, in such an environment, for an employee to find meaning in his or her work? From another point of view, is a company more effective by developing strong values, being engaged to develop meaning, and working to reach its essentials? We have observed that some organizations have invested a lot of their energy in bringing meaning to their activity. We wanted to understand these effects.

The ways we chose

For over 50 years, the quality movement experienced the richness of cultural confrontation. Thanks to its contributions, we stay convinced that the innovation power present inside diversity constitutes a first lead. And so, we decided to explore this world that moved in a new way.

Still we tried to avoid two traps. The first one was the use of well-known experts of our time, whom we knew would only demonstrate that what they observed corresponded to their own field of expertise. The second one was the butterfly effect—seeing only those who wish to be seen.

The contribution of Summer Camps

We decided to bring together men and women who experienced successful change, no matter the field of activity: private or public, lucrative or not, famous or not. The choice was established based on serendipity, following chance opportunities and meetings.

We brought these people together in groups of 50, for five days each time. Three simple rules were to be respected:

- The sessions were long on purpose, in a world where every single minute matters, especially for a chief executive officer.

- There was no program, precisely because, in a world based on consumption, you want to be sure that it will be worth your money.

- It was free, precisely because, today, without a profit goal, it's not serious.

We named these sessions "Summer Camps," never thinking this name would one day become famous.

Fourteen Summer Camps took place, bringing together more than thirty nationalities from five continents. Never once appeared the will to demonstrate or to sell an idea or concept. The only point was to confront experiences and to welcome anything that would emerge.

The various companies on which this book is based have lived the adventure of the Summer Camps several times. This slow maturation allowed the birth of the points described in the second section of this book. They're actually more a sign of biological maturation than of a scientific one, where the intuition, the art, and the joy of living together were as important as the confrontation of practices.

The contribution of the cultural melting pot

From the very beginning, Summer Camps brought together research centers from various cultures—from Europe, Japan, the United States, Africa, and Australia—carried by men and women who themselves went through deep personal and professional change.

Feeling the paradigm change, we didn't want to follow a process that would have prevented us from the needed perspective or the correctness in the analysis. However, we took note of the participants' practices. Among them can be quoted:

- The quality approach, which includes the measure and the resolution of problems

- Semantics, which constructs the link between reality and the idea we have of it

- Behavior sciences and everything we've learned from them in past years

- Beauty, as a means to link man to what's essential

- The Kawakita principles (the 360° observation, the stepping stone, and the role of chance and luck)

All of these wisdoms were not prescribed, but were at the group's disposal to be implemented when the time was right.

The Summer Camps created an open community of men and women, bringing together 200 to 300 people from 30 different countries to create a community rich from their experience and diversity, united by the perception that they were part of something really fundamental. This diversity permitted reflections to evolve: reflections on change, reflections on the search for the essential, and even reflections on reconciliation, when everything seems to divide (for example, in areas where different communities fought.) For five years, they made the content of this book blossom.

The content of the book
This book is divided into two sections.

The first section contains interviews with the visionary leaders of several European businesses. It reflects the words of these leaders whose companies served as examples of transformation. It is their story, in their own words. It will allow each and every one of us to learn what we need, depending on our culture and position of observation.

The second section of this book has two chapters that introduce the problems of managing the rapid rate of change in today's globalized world, and then three chapters discussing eight principles for visionary leadership in this rapidly changing, globalized world.

The two sections of the book are complementary but there may also be some redundancy. (They both deal with several of the same companies.) These two sections are the result of related but not closely coordinated projects; we hope any overlap provides the reader with greater insight by showing somewhat different points of view. Readers might view the first (interview) section as containing the raw data, albeit beautifully described and digested, and the second section as an analysis partially drawn from the data of the first section.

We now invite you to enter and read this information, which explores transformation and will undoubtedly provide you with a few leads to enlighten your own transformational change.

—Bertrand Jouslin de Noray, Secretary General of EOQ

Section One

Case Studies

Elisabeth Ballery

Chapter One

FAVI:
Compassion for Clients

FAVI

Activity: Copper alloy injection (foundry)

Location: Hallencourt, France

Creation: 1957

Manpower: 600 people

Turnover: 66 million euros, of which 35% are exports

Exportation countries: Eastern Europe, European Union, South America, United States

Formation: 9% of the total staff

First European foundry to get ISO 14001 certification in 1997

First French foundry to get OHSAS 18001 certification in 2000

First copper alloy foundry to get ISO/TS 16949 and ISO 9001 certification

FAVI has adhered to the U.N. Global Compact since January 2004.

As Jean-François Zobrist, one morning in April 1983, climbs into a helicopter behind "the Great Max," little does he know that nothing could have prepared him for what is to come. Impassioned with parachuting and flying, he enjoys the landscape that unfolds before him. The pilot, a man he knows well, is the boss for whom he has worked since 1966: Max Rousseaux, more familiarly called "the Great Max."

Odd character, this Great Max, a captain of industry who came to light during the post-war period, first by collecting, in the scarcity context of that time, old jerrycans, and then sheets made of steel, aluminium, or magnesium, left behind by the American army. Understanding that the country would be in short supply of steel, he and some associates create PUM, a company that is concerned not only with supplying the metal desperately needed during the post-war period, but also with rolling it, cutting it to size, cleaning it, and galvanizing it. PUM's motto is "providing service ahead of time."

Set up a metal refinery!

In 1966, one of PUM's general managers informs the Great Max that France's last metal refiner will be closing its doors. Thinking that this situation need not be an obstacle, the Great Max reacts by saying, "If there's nobody left to satisfy the French market, there has to be money to be made. Let's set up a metal refinery." So was born AFICA (Affinage Champagne Ardennes– Champagne Ardennes Refinery), near Reims.

Jean-François Zobrist, fresh from military service and holding a metalwork diploma, is hired to create AFICA's analysis laboratory. Just 22 years old, he persuades the Great Max to invest 500,000 francs in a sparkle spectro, while the company's capital amounts to just 400,000 francs. This piece of equipment, demonstrates the young man in the boss' office, can analyze the amount of copper before ingots are cast, which would put an end to the arduous task of sampling a few ingots after fabrication to determine their copper content. Moreover, this solution offers the advantage of correcting the baths to get a final product that is as close as possible to the parameters clients want.

"Are you sure this equipment works?" questions the Great Max, before abruptly adding, "You look like a good fellow; go ahead."

"So was Max!" recalls Zobrist, years later. "He would test, weigh up, and judge men. And then, relying on intuition, he would or wouldn't trust. We were allowed to make mistakes, under two conditions: being honest and being truthful."

The enthroning

Between 1966 and 1983, Zobrist devotes himself at AFICA to the improvement of alloys, according to the demand of clients, and starts traveling in France and abroad—first for technical-assistance purposes, then for prospecting and selling. In the early seventies, FAVI (Fonderie et Ateliers du Vimeu), one of AFICA's clients, is caught in financial difficulties, and the Great Max decides to buy the company from Picardie. He asks Zobrist to drop in at FAVI from time to time to "conduct a sort of marketing with those he considered excellent technicians, but poor tradesmen."

In the early eighties, Dominique, head of FAVI, announces he is leaving the company to pursue a career in plastics injection. Zobrist is charged with finding his successor. He suggests several candidates, but the Great Max turns down all of them.

On the April 1983 morning mentioned at the beginning of this case study, the Great Max summons him into his office in Reims. First he gives him a $20 gold coin and tells him it might bring him luck. Then he gives him a book written by Auguste Detoeuf, *Tellings of O.L. Barenton, Confectioner*, a classic from the thirties about the adventures and reflections of a manufacturer in the aftermath of World War I, such as: "It's not complicated in a factory to do what's necessary, but it's by doing what's superfluous that you make money. Treat men like machines, and they produce what's necessary; treat them like men, and maybe you will get the superfluous." Then, without any further ado, Max says, "Follow me!" and leads Zobrist to the helicopter. Destination: FAVI.

On the grass just outside of the factory, Dominique awaits them. "Call the staff together," orders the Great Max. Then, in front of a hundred people, he says: "Dominique has done a great job. Now he wants to go. He has earned the right; let him go." And, turning to Zobrist, he declares: "Here is his successor!"

"Without any further comment," recalls Zobrist, "he climbed back into the helicopter, whose blades began to move again. I found myself alone with Dominique, facing the employees, with my book about Barenton in one hand and my golden coin in the other, and I realized that something important had just happened. Dominique asked me if I had expected it, to which I answered, 'No, absolutely not!' I had a flat in Reims, had convinced my aging parents-in-law to buy a flat on the same floor, my daughter was going to school in Reims, my wife worked there, and I was president and an instructor at my parachute club in Reims. I had never considered leaving Reims!"

That's the way Zobrist was enthroned as head of FAVI.

First step: Doing nothing for four months

Taken aback by what had happened—"I had never once imagined that I would one day get the chance and opportunity to oversee such a fine company," he recalls, still amazed—Zobrist makes a deal with Dominique. Dominique would remain in charge until the end of July. Zobrist, meanwhile, would do nothing but observe. For four months, the leader-to-be does just that. He notices all the distinctive features of a well-managed seventies-era factory:

▶ An office on the top floor, with a window overlooking the whole factory.

- A timekeeper, and a regulation that a worker's arriving five minutes late results in five minutes cut from the paycheck, being 10 minutes late, 10 minutes cut, etc.

- A locked storage area.

- A coin-operated drink dispenser. During the summer months, employees receive free tokens for the machine. They must obtain these tokens from the switchboard.

- A purchases service, a staff service, a planning function, a regulator, a supervisor, shop foremen, chiefs of staff, and departmental managers.

- A daily ceremony for the opening of mail by the management team.

- A management board, executive officers' meetings, planning meetings, and meetings for solving the quality problems encountered during the previous month.

- Monthly bonuses, including a quality bonus, a produced tons bonus, an attendance bonus, and a foundry heat bonus.

- At regular intervals in the various workshops, short-time working at the end of the month, to maintain the pressure.

"In short," comments Zobrist, "everything was there to make a company work, and it worked well. The deadlines of that time were respected, the quality standards at that time were suitable, and the company made a small profit. In all likelihood, had I run the company just as Dominique had, things would have stayed the same, especially since neither the employees nor management wished for them to change. The specifications of the former boss had been very simple and true to his philosophy: 'Make me earn money and don't go to prison!' In his lively and manly language, this meant: 'You have full discretion to act as you see fit, as long as it is legal.'"

During his four months of observation, Zobrist is followed everywhere by the workshop foreman while he takes his daily tour of the factory. This goes on until the day when, exasperated by this little game, Zobrist organizes a meeting with all of the managers and says: "I perfectly understand that every last one of you has made your service or your workshop your own. But what you fail to see is that I made the factory my own once I arrived. The whole place is now mine." The situation gets better, however, once the managers see that Zobrist takes the time during each of his walks around the factory to chat with the workers, asking them such things as where they live and how many children they have, in an effort to get to know them better.

Rather quickly, Zobrist makes a number of important observations:

▪ When a worker needs a new pair of gloves, he/she shows his/her worn gloves to the foreman, who gives the worker a ticket. The worker goes to the locked storage area, rings, waits for the attendant to come, and, in exchange for the ticket, gets a pair of new gloves. The whole operation takes a good 10 minutes. Meanwhile, the cost of the machine the worker works on is 10 francs per minute, while the gloves cost only 5.80 francs. "This makes that pair of gloves that one must get from the locked storage area awfully expensive," mentally notes Zobrist.

▪ The same goes for coffee: Since there is only one dispenser in the whole factory, workers lose from three to five minutes of productivity for each cup of coffee they get—which means that one cup costs between 30 and 50 francs.

▪ During the meetings addressing failures in quality standards of the previous month, the problems discussed are weeks old. Nobody remembers them anymore, least of all the workers, who have since encountered new problems.

▪ The daily mail-opening ceremony isn't very useful either, since 95% of the letters don't pertain to management. But when the boss isn't there, everyone waits for his return to open the mail.

▶ During weekly meetings, the managers spend their time settling their scores in front of the boss, trying to explain why they didn't adhere to the planning of the past week. As a result, only a few minutes of the meetings are spent discussing the week to come.

▶ When the evening comes, the rush toward the timekeeper starts, and frequently some workers wait in the area for the bell to ring so they can punch out quickly.

▶ In addition, notes Zobrist, "I noticed that the boss spent over a day each month calculating, with each manager, the monthly bonus for their staff. I told myself that the bonus based on the produced tonnage was rather unfair, since the workers had nothing to do with the amount of tons to be produced. I also realized that the heat bonus, created for the foundry during the summer months, was ridiculous: It doesn't get less hot because you give extra money to the metal founders. I noticed that founders tended to close the windows when the weather was hot, because the bonus was proportional to the heat measured in the workshop! Last but not least, I observed that workers were sad, frequently looked at the clocks in the workshops, and almost ran to get out of work at the end of the day."

The tale of the lawn mower

Zobrist takes good note of everything he observes in the factory. At the same time, however, he feels a little discouraged because, as he explains, "I had no alternatives to propose for the most serious matters." He searches in vain for ideas for solutions by reviewing the classes he took at the CNAM in Reims. He then discovers a formation organization in Paris, called the AFPIMM, where he seeks answers. There he learns about statistical process control (SPC), Kanban, total productive maintenance (TPM), social dynamism, and various company projects. Zobrist also meets Jean-Christian Fauvet, vice president of the famous business-consultancy practice Bossard. Still, at that moment, Zobrist doesn't know what to do with the information he has just learned or with his new contact.

The end of July approaches, and a party is thrown at FAVI for Dominique's departure. As the day comes to a close, Zobrist still has no idea how he will initiate the needed changes in this firm. He plans to dedicate his vacation time to settling his family in Picardie—until the day his lawn mower shows signs of breakdown.

Just a week before going back to work, Zobrist begins to mow his lawn. But soon the motor starts misfiring. He takes a wrench, dismantles the spark plug, realizes that the electrodes are sooted up, cleans them, puts the spark plug back together, and resumes mowing the lawn. The misfirings have stopped. He proceeds with his task, proud to have found the solution at once and to have totally solved the problem.

Then he starts wondering: How would this problem be solved at the factory? Petrified, he realizes that the following chain reaction would take place: The worker, who has no right to intervene directly, would call the regulator. The regulator, realizing after a few tries that it's not a setting problem but a maintenance problem, would give notice to the workshop foreman, who in turn would warn the chief of staff, who is the only one with the capacity of notifying the chief of maintenance. A mechanic would then be sent, would clean the carburetor just in case, and, concluding that the problem still wasn't rectified, would notify the electrician. Then, at last, the electrician would dismantle the spark plug and go to the locked storage area to ask for a new one (because a "real" professional doesn't waste time cleaning a spark plug). And the same chain reaction would then occur in reverse to verify that everything was back in place.

Zobrist is stunned. How will he allow workers at FAVI to repair their own machines? "Unknowingly," he explains afterward, "this incident made me understand that for the company to be reactive, decisions had to be made by the workers themselves, in real time. I realized that good workers are those who take initiative, just as they do all the time at home. The manufacturing process was there only to rule out any worker initiative. This structure had to be suppressed, or at least reoriented toward other goals."

The first symbolic decisions

During his first day back at work after vacation, the question of "how" is still a mystery for Zobrist. For lack of a global method, he decides to "make it while moving forward" (an expression borrowed from Picardie, meaning "make things happen first, and think about consequences later"). He starts changing the most settled and symbolic routines at FAVI. He suppresses the daily mail ceremony and asks the accountant to distribute it from that point on. "I noticed very quickly that I was better informed than before," he says. "Since everybody knew I no longer oversaw all the mail, individuals came to tell me about pertinent information during my daily factory tour. Before, I used to read some of the letters over people's shoulders without getting their real message."

Then Zobrist has the window of his office—the one that makes it possible to supervise the workshop from above—bricked up. He also stops attending the weekly planning meetings in an effort to limit the settling of scores between chiefs of staff, and he suppresses the Monday-morning managers meetings, which he comments "was mostly designed to settle my position."

The search for a new management system

After making these changes, Zobrist comes to a major realization: The whole organizational chart betrays an assumption that man is bad. "He's considered a thief, since all the supplies are locked up; lazy, since he is given cadences; stupid, since there are methods in place to do all the thinking for him; and unconscientious, since there are supervisors," he explains. "But the supervisors themselves are not considered to be very serious since there is another, higher level of supervision, which is also lax since there is an expedition supervisor. It gave me an idea of the road I needed to follow. I imagined another organizational chart that considered man is good, because people always end up being the way you consider them."

Understanding that systems help to shape the people who work within them, he searches for a new system for FAVI that is likely to make its workers evolve. Lessons he learned from the AFPIMM begin to take effect.

Zobrist compares two models, for instance. One is that of Company X, which devotes most of its energy to protecting itself against anything negative that might happen. Always in search of a state of zero risk, staff members make every effort to edict rules that end up paralyzing the system to the point where the company is no longer able to fix any problems.

Another model is that of Company Y, which ignores what might happen tomorrow and concentrates its energy on what is happening now. As soon as a problem occurs, a network is created to address it, and the network is dissolved once the problem is fixed. The firm emphasizes freedom for everyone, limited only by a few simple rules and values.

As a consequence, risk taking, even if it results in failure, is not penalized. When it comes to the benefit of the client, every power is given to the operators, for they are the ones working to solve the clients' problems. The boss, meanwhile, is not directly involved. Instead, he/she acts as a coach, seated on the sidelines, observing and scrutinizing to see what is happening and making an effort to support the rest of the team.

Startled by the good sense of this model, Zobrist summons all the managers at FAVI, explains his conclusions, and asks: "What if we considered that man is good?" His ideas are met with resistance. As he explains, "I realized I couldn't expect their consensus. I would have to provoke, alone, a real, brutal, irreversible breakthrough. I also realized I had to lean on another 'caste,' since the managers believed they had everything to lose!"

The breakthrough

Just before the Christmas break, Zobrist brings the whole staff together. He then announces, to the stupefied assembly, several breakthrough changes that will occur after the Christmas break: dismantling of the timekeeper, removal of the end-of-day bell, and suppression of the delay penalty system—since a delay can be completely justified for technical or personal reasons. "You are not paid to make time, but to make steel pieces, good pieces," he declares.

He then announces he is doing away with the bonus and replacing it with the average of what each worker received over the past two years, a sum that will be integrated into his or her salaries. The locked storage door is to be dismantled, and the storage area will now be a place that can be easily accessed by all, with the only obligation being to write on a board what has been taken so that it can be restocked in a timely manner. The paying drinks dispenser will be replaced by two free dispensers located in each workshop. Several measures will also be instated regarding locating sets of tools close to the workstations. Finally, Zobrist announces the suppression of the systematic short-time working periods.

The head of FAVI then explains the company's new principles of management, which he dares to compare to those of a streetwalker! First: She has to look attractive to her clients, and FAVI has to as well. Second: She wears some makeup to be noticed. Inside the FAVI building, machines will be clean and painted in bright colors. Comments Zobrist: "This replaced the thinking of that time, when cleaning a machine was considered a loss of time that could be spent working. We used this second principle instead of the lean-enterprise 5S method for a few years."

Third principle: A street walker has specialties that attract the client; otherwise, both of them would stay home. Zobrist's translation for FAVI: "We are only producing pieces of rough cast. We will try to tool them, fit them together, and deliver them. Before that happens, we will try to conceive them, improve them, and test them to try and make the best possible product for our clients." Fourth principle: A street walker doesn't give illnesses to her clients; otherwise, she would lose them all at once.

"We needed to cure ourselves of three major diseases," Zobrist continues. "The first one was delivery delays. It's an unforgivable illness, because Tuesday isn't Monday. If we promise something for Monday, we have to keep this promise at any cost. Otherwise, it will be impossible to convince our clients that things that aren't immediately evident, such as quality and price, are desirable in our products. Second: How can we prove that our prices are the right ones? I see only one solution: never raise our prices again. And then, one day, inevitably, we will have the best prices in France, and why not in Europe, and why not in the world? The third disease is poor quality standards. And for this one, I had no miracle cure. I told the workers that they are the almighty ones! What management can do, back in our offices, is listen to them and try to help. But workers must be aware that they, and they alone, on their machines, can do everything."

First results

The transformation process was now under way! With two principles—"make it while moving forward" and "man is good"—in hand, Zobrist launched his irreversible process of change, leaving no possibility for a U-turn. And the process soon resulted, to his utter surprise, with results that went far beyond his expectations.

After workers had returned from Christmas break, against all odds (since bonuses had been suppressed), cadences began to increase. The best performance was registered by FAVI's female operators, who produced as much as 20% more pieces per hour. Little by little, Zobrist solved this mystery: These workers had taken on a rhythm that was faster, physiologically optimum, and less demanding in energy. When he asked them why they hadn't done this before, since it would have enabled them to earn more money from bonuses, they replied, "We're not crazy! Had we done that, we would not have received any bonuses because the supervisors would have raised the quota of pieces we needed to produce."

Another noticeable positive effect became evident: Before, at quitting time, all the staff was lined up in front of the timekeeper, eager to leave for the day. Now, at quitting time, everyone was still at his/her workstation, and when the evening came, it wasn't unusual to see some workers staying 15 minutes late to finish up their work.

The schedule for delivery to clients was absolutely respected. One day, however, it almost wasn't. A young woman in charge of sending deliveries had forgotten to arrange for transportation for some pieces that had to be delivered the same day in Brittany. Zobrist reacted by saying, "It doesn't matter!" and calling for a helicopter to ship part of the delivery, thus proving that the rule was unfailing. The client's reaction: "We saw a helicopter land, full of metal pieces from your firm! You're insane; a delay of one day wouldn't have mattered."

"It's not really for you that I rented the helicopter," answered Zobrist. "It's for us, to prove that we can never be late to deliver." In 2004, the company's service rate (percentage of complete deliveries honored on time) had gone up to 99.97%.

Little by little, FAVI's new system comes to shape. With team members being less cautious thanks to the results obtained with Zobrist's first measures, the model of FAVI is conceived, close to that of the aforementioned Company Y: no management board, staff services, ground management, planning, sales services, technical supervisors, timekeeper, or bonuses. At the core are shared values, "sort of a modern translation of the ancestral notion of common good," comments Zobrist. These shared values include basic safety rules, fabrication process, respect for quality and the environment, plus a few comportmental rules: honesty, good sense, good will, and good mood.

"If and only if our clients love FAVI, then they will be willing to pay the money needed for the firm to last," says Zobrist. And how will FAVI last? "By selling pieces of steel the clients will like better than those from our rivals," is the answer. The FAVI system is able to help operators evolve—one no longer differentiates between "workers" and "management" because inside FAVI everyone is a worker, meaning that everyone works for the client. This concept is illustrated by the symbols in FAVI's new logo: A tree, which symbolizes the lasting quality of the company; a heart, which symbolizes the love clients feel for FAVI; and a circle, which symbolizes the bringing together of operators and clients.

The creation of mini-factories

As time passes, a human dilemma must be settled—a consultant recommends that Zobrist fire a chief of machining, whose department has grown from 10 to 80 workers but who can rule only a 10-person department—and the model gets even richer. Zobrist and the consultant brainstorm answers to the question "How can we bring the number of people under the direct authority of this man under 10?"

That's when the concept of mini-factories was devised. It constitutes the structuring of the whole firm into small, 10-person, autonomous groups, each of them dedicated to one particular client or product. Each group has a team leader who, together with his/her team, manages the orders and the manufacturing.

Besides allowing Zobrist to avoid firing the foretold chief, this solution enabled FAVI to reach the goals Zobrist had always pursued on intuition: to build a model that would give importance to the operators and establish a unique manufacturing structure with only two hierarchical levels–operators and their team leaders. Managers and executive officers thus act as experts in their fields of competence and are devoted to the minifactories and, of course, to the clients.

This progressive shaping of FAVI's model illustrates once more the sacred principle of "make it while moving forward"—which leads, with no fear of risk, to the adoption of the most inventive solutions, one problem at a time, and theorizing only afterward. Another one of Zobrist's formulas describes this state of mind: "Act for today; think 20 years from now."

Acting for today is prudent because operators need to solve their problems immediately. And thinking 20 years from now (not three or six months from now, or a year from now, as is often the case in industry) is prudent because it's not acceptable to worry only about the current annual budget. The perpetuity of the firm requires a permanent adaptation to clients' needs and tastes. Thus, making a decision to invest in a new machine isn't a problem. Says Zobrist: "Fifteen minutes is enough time for making an investment decision. We don't stop to evaluate the risks or to calculate the amortization of the machine depending on obtaining a contract. While you take the time to do all the math, you lose your reactivity to your clients; hence you lose new contract opportunities."

From 1983 to 2006, FAVI has been managed according to those values and principles. The company has seen major growth, jumping from 100 to 600 employees. It has become a leader in the field of copper alloy injection. Its wire forks equip one out of every two European cars made.

Over the past 20 years, the company has been able to integrate Japanese methods to improve productivity and performance. (These methods have also been adopted by other companies worldwide.) This is thanks to trips to Japan that Zobrist made with a man named Bernard, an operator and former agricultural worker who is gifted with much common sense and a passion for new methods. Bernard particularly appreciated the Japanese methods and the respect they have for the comfort of the operators while they do their work. FAVI has adopted the most up-to-date methods.

In January 2004, Zobrist's successor was appointed: A man named Dominique, who was originally hired at FAVI with only a technical diploma in hand. He is determined to perpetuate the model he has witnessed for 20 years. Today, Zobrist, now 62, devotes himself to the development of high-performance engines, a key market in the worldwide effort to counteract the greenhouse effect. FAVI holds a strong position within this market thanks to an innovation that it is the only company in the world to hold!

How was it possible that this transformation process worked so well and was never questioned externally? Zobrist explains: "The system of 'make it while moving forward,' where everyone takes initiative and does what he/she believes to be right, all the while framed by a strong value system, proved to be powerful! I'm astonished when a high-ranking representative of a car manufacturer decides to visit us but first must check to see if there is a company car available on that date. The weight of policies in organizations is dreadful. At FAVI, all our cars are available for anyone who needs them. Clients have seen our operators arrive at their sites in our most beautiful company cars, because our rule is that the more kilometers you drive, the more comfortable the car you take."

Zobrist has never doubted the value of the transformation process. "I have a huge flaw: I can't bear stupid things that go against common sense, such as closing the windows when it's hot because there's a heat bonus. I don't have any notion of risk, which allows me to go forward and think freely. That's why I found Picardie's concept of 'make it while moving forward' so easy to adopt. Thanks to this method, and to the interest I have in mankind, all my company leaders are former wage earners, while at any other company they would have remained in such jobs forever. This system is simple: You take the best person at one key moment, to answer one precise need. And it works!"

"Without a particularly outstanding course, we steadily grew from 100 employees to 600 in 20 years, while at the same time having a good life and rewarding our shareholders. This, of course, triggered the following remark: 'It's because you're a healthy company that you can afford such a structure.' But, to the contrary, it's only because we work in a permanent state of happiness, a happiness brought on by our method, that it works so well."

Zobrist certainly gets his love for mankind from his education and from his culture, but it also comes from the people he has met, including Max Rousseaux, Jean-Christian Fauvet, and many others. Well before he became the head of FAVI, when he was still taking courses at the CNAM, a reflection from one of his professors regarding work organization made a deep impression on him: "Don't forget that behind everything are human beings."

Zobrist knows the sustainability of the FAVI system is due mostly to the family base of the enterprise's shareholders. Today FAVI is the property of the Great Max's widow. Also reassuring is the fact that the family's grandchildren are very interested by FAVI's new innovation and high-performance engine.

Zobrist is nevertheless conscious of the frailty of this system: "I'm deeply convinced that the company's performance comes from the operators themselves and that, deep down, it's all about two or three differences between us and our rivals. But if our system, which was built step by step, were to crumble—in the event of an acquisition, for example—it would be over."

What does Zobrist think, then, of the evolution of European, North American, and world industry? The car industry obviously reacts in the opposite way from his famous "act for today, think 20 years from now" formula.

"What happens today with China is pure nonsense," he remarks. "Today, European subcontractors invoice competitive products that integrate the most severe social and environmental constraints. Manufacturers, however, choose to get supplies from China, where those constraints are not followed. But what prices will they get tomorrow on the Chinese market? Of course, when that time comes, there will be no European or North American subcontractors anymore—nor car manufacturers, for that matter! We already know that, by 2010, China will be producing twice its need in cars."

Zobrist can't do anything but marvel at the newfound infatuation journalists and theorists have for the model created by FAVI. "The trauma surrounding General Motors is huge in the United States. Until now, Americans were conscious that their management system had been adopted worldwide. Now, they realize they have crashed into the wall. Followers of capitalism, which involves the respect of certain rules, are left behind by a brutal form of capitalism, like the one that reigns in China. As a consequence, they become worried and look for new management models.

"What surprises them is that in France, a company has succeeded in building the most liberal system imaginable. And, thanks to our structure—or lack thereof—FAVI manages to stay more competitive than its Chinese rivals. This seems to demonstrate that, when you work differently, it is possible to last."

Chapter Two

SOL: The Sunny Company

SOL

Activity: Business-to-business cleaning services (80% of the activity); Facility and property maintenance services (10%); Laundry and dry cleaning services (10%)

Location: Helsinki, Finland

Creation: 1848/1991

Manpower: 7200 people (5500 in Finland, 1300 in Estonia, 400 in Latvia, and a few employees in Russia and Poland)

Turnover 2005: 118 million euros

Trading results: 6% to 10% of the turnover since 1993

Formation: 2% of the turnover

ISO 9000:2000, ISO 14001, and OHSAS 18001 certified

Winner of the "Excellence Finland Award" in 1991 and 1993

You can't avoid it. It's everywhere. On the employees' caps, on the envelopes, on the investigations about customer satisfaction. What is it? A sun. A bright yellow sun, highlighted with red, staring at its interlocutor with a beautiful smile in the same color. The company's logo? It's a lot more than that. It's a trademark, and the sign of a rebirth for this company, created in 1848, completely recast between 1991 and 1993 by Liisa Joronen. The concrete mark also, of a dream come true...

A dream and a family conflict

But let's go back to the sources of SOL. The company has its roots in one of Finland's oldest enterprises. In 1848, M. Lindstrom opens a small dyeing workshop in Helsinki. Soon, he diversifies his activities into laundry and dry cleaning. In the early 1900s, Johan Roiha, Liisa Joronen's grandfather, buys the company and expands it into a laundry service. Liisa's father, Eino Roiha, brings textile rental into the business in the sixties. Then, in the seventies, the development of cleaning activities brings Lindstrom (the company has kept its creator's name) into a new era, that of businesspeople.

Liisa had decided at a very young age to become the leader of the family company. In 1981 she was appointed managing director of Lindstrom. "There are several ways of leading a company. In a family business, in particular, the holder's values and conceptions have a lot of influence on the culture and way of management. But my values and my idea of the company's evolution were very different from those shared by my whole family," she comments.

At that time, Liisa already had a dream—a dream of a company where employees would be proud of themselves, where the manpower would take initiatives and would be in direct contact with the customer. She dreamt of a company without superfluous rules, without useless chiefs, without a constraining hierarchical system that prevented wageworkers from doing their job correctly. "I deeply believe that employees work well when they're given the freedom to decide what concerns them daily, better than when their leaders decide for them."

But this dream was the beginning of an inevitable family clash between Liisa and her relatives, who still believed in their methods and practiced management as other companies did.

To dismiss a family quarrel and damages that would go beyond repair for the company, Liisa's father decided in 1991 to break the firm into two parts. Liisa took the cleaning business, nonprofitable at that time, and a small activity of waste management; her brother and three sisters received the laundry and linen-renting part. "I was very happy with that, since I was now able to implement what I was passionate about and to pursue my dream. But I was frantic at the same time; who would agree to follow me, to forsake the reassuring head house to jump into the unknown? What would the employees and the clients decide? And how would we survive without money and with a deficit?"

To add to this context, Finland was at that time in the middle of an economic recession, "the worst of Finland's history. A lot of firms and many employees were going through very difficult times," recalls Liisa. "Fortunately, we were so enthusiastic that we were far from spending our time crying or in fear. We were sure of ourselves, and of our newfound way."

The first signs of transformation

To mark the break with the old structure, changes were first turned toward outer signs, immediately perceptible to clients and employees. The first step: to find a headquarters for this new company. "Because we couldn't afford anything else, we rented an old movie studio that had gone into bankruptcy," tells Liisa. "And at once we started to ask simple questions: Why would we have offices that look like offices? Why work from 9 a.m. to 5 p.m.? That's the way our way of living and working to-gether started taking form. SOL Studio—today SOL City—was created by SOL people, according to their ideas. No less than 1146 suggestions were registered during our brainstorming ses-sions. Our pride was to create something no one had ever seen or dared to dream of. We created workspaces that were closer to a home environment or an imaginary one, than to actual offices. Since then, SOL City and this new work method were met with a huge echo in the media, and we keep receiving visits from all around the world!"

What's so original about SOL City? There, none of the 200 em-ployees has his or her own office, but instead use workspaces that are at their disposal. Before their departure, everything that lies on the desks is tidied away in a portfolio and set in a locker. This is a precise illustration of one of SOL's key principles: what matters is not *where* the work is done, but *how* it is done. This principle can be embodied in a corollary: total freedom in work hours. A mission can be done at home, at night, or on the week-end if it's easier for the workers, and they only come to the office when they choose to.

A nice and cheerful decoration, bright colors—just like a cir-cus—support two other major principles at SOL: creativity and happiness at work. But let there be no mistake! The disposition of these workspaces, although ravishing, costs only one third of a classic one. "If you integrate communication fees and the price of employees journeys to their workplaces (that are charged to the company), it climbs up to half of the cost of a regular disposi-tion," according to the general manager, Anu Eronen.

Long-lasting symbols

A second evolution, full of meaning, was the search for a new name for the company. "We launched a contest within every agency and for every employee. We received 1200 proposals.

Among them, we chose SOL, which means sun, light, positive spirit, and happiness at work." From this name came the company's new color—yellow. "It's a color that also represents creativity and courage," adds Liisa. "This new name and these new offices became the support of our new way of working and of our collective dream."

"Since then," Liisa goes on, "I've worn yellow every day. Not once have I gone to work or to a professional meeting without wearing yellow outfits. Most of my sport or casual clothes are yellow too, from my swimming suit to my evening dress. I have often found myself in the middle of 2000 people wearing black at a party, and me, alone, dressed in luminous yellow. It's my way of showing my employees and the world that I'm proud of this company and that I have faith in us to achieve what we promise to do."

Constantly reaffirmed values

"Then," explains Liisa, "we rapidly created other studios for our locations in Finland. Employees of each agency always conceive and realize their own studio. Our 40 other locations are all different, yet similar, because they share a common concept that makes SOL's workspaces unique. We don't have any rules concerning the aspects of these workspaces; they just have to reflect the company's philosophy." This philosophy relies on the following values: freedom, responsibility, trust, creativity, happiness at work, and learning throughout life. It also relies on the fundamental principle of a positive view of man. "We believe that everyone wishes to do good work. Each employee has thus to be appreciated, recognized, and independent in his or her work. Everybody proves to be creative daily, even if we're all different."

The management and the company's methods had to be in harmony with this philosophy. From the start, SOL's leitmotivs were: to avoid bureaucracy, to show the path with a few big goals, to allow the employees themselves to follow up on these goals by giving them the means to obtain immediate input from the customers, and to engage all employees, thanks to the pleasure they experience in doing their work and in satisfying clients. "Our pride today is to bring together people who both love their work and their clients," rejoices Liisa.

The building of SOL's model of management: "The happy work revolution"

Those few leading principles, which fit Liisa's initial dream and her strong intuition, were progressively formalized in a series of unavoidable points that summarize the happy work revolution that took place within SOL:

▶ The freedom to work when, where, and how the workers wish, as long as they reach their goals and fulfill the needs of the clients. Cleaning agents decide on their schedule with their clients. Every agency, and most employees, have cell phones, voice mail, laptops, and all of the necessary materials to work when and where they wish. This new system permits a great improvement in daily relations with customers.

▶ No inner regulation, hierarchical titles, or advantages linked to status—no secretary, no function car, no dedicated rooms or offices. Each employee has a clear vision of his/her perimeter of action and responsibilities, and knows he/she has to contribute to the lasting and well-being of service to the clients (for example, during colleagues' holidays or absence).

▶ A total transparency of the company's results. Each month, employees receive updated financial information and data on clients' satisfaction, etc.

- The conceptualization of the offices naturally eliminates any territorial claim or advantage linked to a function. Employees use any workspace available when they arrive. When the work is done, they clean the zone for others to take their place. This measure, as well as every other, applies to every employee, including leadership.

- Implementation of goals, defined by the employees themselves. Because employees are naturally ambitious, their own goals correspond to a high degree of demand.

- Establishment of payment integrating a fixed half, with the second half being linked to the reaching of goals.

- Willing participation in the numerous formations. A homemade exam, established by the employees with the help of external consultants, concerns eight modules: basic education, customer department, communication, "sunny service," marketing, productivity and efficiency, accountability, and performance. The time of education for each module lasts several months. Several hundred agents thus received education from a tutor.

To all those points must be added a quality management element, in which SOL invested a lot in surveillance, research, and even applied research. The company ordered, for example, a study on customer satisfaction from a university. Thanks to these works, SOL was able to create its own satisfaction barometer ("the joy barometer"), which it applies several times a year. SOL also measures the satisfaction of the clients in five different ways; a simple evaluation of the satisfaction is made each month with clients. Cleaning agents themselves make half of the 20,000 studies in face-to-face discussions. Moreover, cleaning agents implement, once a year, the 28,000 quality audits. Several other studies and investigations are accomplished by the company, a sort of "listening to the client," to know what direction the company should take to maintain a high level of satisfaction among its clients and a high level of profit. "There's not a single day that passes by without discussions about the client's satisfaction and the way we could still improve our services," summarizes Liisa.

Outstanding results

The dream came true. In accordance with her first intuitions, Liisa's philosophy was very well received by the clients. Without any announcements or TV advertisements, SOL rapidly became a well-known brand for the originality of its management model and its excellent results. Clients' satisfaction climbed to a very high level as soon as the first transformations took place. From the start, the company went back to high profitability—one of the best in Finland—with the same excellent level of client satisfaction.

How can this miracle be explained? Studies of the companies revealed one crucial point: the close link between the satisfaction of the clients, the employees, and the level of profit. In other words, happy workers make happy customers but moreover faithful ones and a profitable business! Especially in a service activity where wageworkers represent 90% of the total costs. "Those employees who are close to their clients and have total autonomy to act and make decisions are happier in their work, and thus bring the best service to the client. Work has taken on a new dimension. Each day proves that a lot of problems can be solved in the field, before they become difficulties or customer claims. The SOL example shows that when employees are truly independent, they don't need managers or leaders. They can do most of the management themselves," analyzes Liisa.

This company, now famous in Finland, has become highly attractive for employees. SOL never encountered any recruiting problems, even when the market for the cleaning sector became highly difficult. Their turnover rate is low. Many employees have worked for the company for 10 years, which is extremely rare in this field of activity. The functioning of the company is particularly adapted to people who, for personal reasons, wish to adapt their schedule and to choose their working hours.

With these excellent results, SOL quickly enlarged its activities to facility and property maintenance services, and in 2001, bought back the laundry services part of the head house. Then, in the same period, SOL started to expand internationally ("the sunny world conquest"). Today the company has 1300 employees in Estonia, 400 in Latvia, and a few in Russia and Poland. The future of the family company is completely safe: Liisa divided 90% of her shares between her three children. Her daughter, Peppi, leads the laundry activities. This firm, which represents 62 dry cleaning shops, is now scheduled to be developed in Finland and in foreign countries. And her son, Juhapekka, has taken on the head of international responsibilities.

When you ask Liisa if the reality is close to the dream she imagined some 20 years ago, the answer is "yes" without a second thought. SOL is now one of the most famous companies in the service sector. It also reached an unmatched level of quality in services, which contributes to its outstanding image. And SOL is in good standing on the international side. And while Liisa recognizes that a lot has already been done, she immediately declares that a lot of challenges are yet to be met in the future. "SOL now has the possibility to become an international service society. For younger generations, the whole world is open and the sky is the only limit."

Where did Liisa find her never-ending energy to build her dream and leave behind any obstacle on her road? To this question she answers with a very simple process, a permanent questioning: "Why, why, why? Management models are so deeply anchored that very few people question their finality or true efficiency," explains Liisa. "The only answer you get when asking this is 'it has always been this way and always will be.' But when you start dismantling the model piece by piece—why are there so many chiefs and managers in most companies, why do all offices look like offices, why do we measure the time we spend working instead of measuring the results—then the 'happy work revolution' can start." Even more advances result when workers are invited to express themselves on the new principles that replace the old system. "We departed from ourselves. These new principles were easy to apply because they were issued from the manpower." Another of Liisa's favorite expressions reveals a lot about her: "Kill routine before it kills you."

Liisa also found energy in the conflict with her family. It could have been destructive, but it proved a great stimulation for Liisa, making her even more determined to show that the model and the company she dreamt of could come true. This strength and determination is incredibly evident in her decision to wear, each day and no matter the circumstance, yellow outfits—the color of her company—to pay tribute to all of her collaborators. But also to prove, to those close to her and to herself, that she will never forsake her fight for her convictions—convictions that are as strong as the profit level and the walls of SOL City.

Chapter Three

St. Charles Medical Center: Healing in a Spirit of Love and Compassion

ST. CHARLES MEDICAL CENTER

Activity: Nonprofit private hospital (240 physicians, 40 medical and surgical specialties)

Location: Two establishments, one in Bend (220 beds) and the other in Redmond (48 beds), Oregon, United States

Creation: 1918

Manpower: 1800 people

"Perhaps it's the triple waterfalls of the Deschutes River. Or the majesty of Mt. Bachelor. Or the quiet elegance of Drake Park. There's something about this part of Oregon that revives the body and restores the spirit," states the booklet that presents the St. Charles Medical Center in Bend, Oregon. In this peaceful landscape, far from any urban center, a medical building, created at the beginning of the last century, could have slowly fallen asleep before completely fading away. But the opposite occurred. This private medical center drew on its assets—an outstanding work environment and a location that provides services to the inhabitants of the local area—to build an inventive care system coupled with medical excellence that stands as a real difference and widens the gap with other care centers in the United States.

A reference in its own area, and one of the best in national classifications

The St. Charles Medical Center was created in Bend in 1918 by the Sisters of St. Joseph, a congregation initially founded in Tipton, Indiana. Although the hospital has not been managed by the Catholic community since the beginning of the seventies, it kept the strong values of attention and compassion that linked it to its origins, as well as its management model: the St. Charles Medical Center is still today a nonprofit private establishment. This is far from implying a lack of performance or a rejection of the competitiveness that prevails today among care centers in the United States. The St. Charles Medical Center stands among the best in the nation for cardiology, oncology, orthopedics, and neurosurgery services. It is regularly quoted among the 100 best establishments in the United States for the quality of its care, its operational efficiency, and its global performance. In the same manner, it has been ranked for several years among the very best hospitals in terms of customer satisfaction.

Today, the St. Charles Medical Center consists of more than 240 physicians and an average of 40 medical and surgical specialties. It has become the hospital of reference for 230,000 people living in central and eastern Oregon. In addition to outstanding surgical services for serious pathologies or operations—open-heart surgery, a level III neonatology center, etc.—the center also possesses specialized analysis laboratories at the regional level, a center for the treatment of cancer, a center dedicated to domestic care, an institute devoted to sleep disorders, and finally, a service for urgent helicopter transportation. The capacity of the hospital rises to 220 beds with a staff of 1800 people.

Since the fifties, the St. Charles Medical Center has also managed a nearby hospital in Redmond, a city located 15 miles north of Bend with a population of 20,000 people. There, some

40 physicians provide obstetrics, gynecology, pediatrics, emergency, general surgery, orthopedics, urology, and other services. The center has beds to accommodate 48 patients. A close collaboration has been established between the teams in Bend and Redmond to provide the most adapted care to patients.

This position of excellence and reference for a whole area was far from being certain only 20 years ago. At that time many people in eastern or central Oregon who were badly injured or victims of heart attacks died during their transfer to Portland, for lack of local high-level care equipment. Even though the state capital city isn't that far away—only 170 miles—ambulances had to travel through the mountains that separate the two cities; that travel time could be fatal to patients in need of emergency care.

The choices for the management of the medical center were simple: to let Bend become a proximity hospital, like the one in Redmond, if no vigorous plan for modernization, equipment, and new specialties was implemented, or to create a pilot care establishment, with a project adapted to the specific geographic location of the hospital. The second option was chosen. Yet, in parallel with the modernization of the hospital and the launching of strong programs to reach a level of national excellence in cardiology, orthopedics, neurosurgery, and cancer treatment, the St. Charles Medical Center knew it had to set some specific values and features that are, today, its originality.

To take care with love and compassion

What precisely are those specific features?

▶ The St. Charles Medical Center opposes individualized care, which is too often delivered in an anonymous and technical way in other hospitals. Even more, the medical staff doesn't separate the medical act itself—which is mainly focused on the body—from the "taking care," which directly touches the individual's mind, dignity, and spirituality. Following this principle, each member of the staff has to implement the mission of the hospital—"to improve the health of those we serve in a spirit of love and compassion." "We know that recovery is due to more than sole technical expertise," states a member of the hospital team.

- The establishment built a model of care, to which any new collaborator is educated and made aware of, with the goal of making a difference for patients. In the course of their careers, members of the staff are invited to improve the technical and clinical aspects of care, as well as their personal relationships with patients. Specific attention is paid to patients that are at the end of their lives, ensuring that they benefit from an adapted environment. The model allows strong choices, in which the medical teams, the medical staff, and even the entire manpower of the hospital find their way. This approach is appreciated by the entire staff and has allowed the center to be recognized for several years by its own workers as one of the 100 best companies to work for in the state of Oregon.

- The global care of the patient—keeping the body united with the comfort of the mind, psychological well-being, and even spiritual inspiration—is provided in several ways. Patients are served by a caring and obliging staff, but also by an important number of volunteers, who improve relations and provide comfort to patients and their family. Staff and volunteers can, for example, bring the mail to the infirmed, help and comfort families in emergency services, ease the pain of patients and their relatives, welcome and receive visitors, organize activities that are adapted to adults suffering from neurodegenerative diseases, and even provide religious services to those who ask for them. Religious services are made possible, no matter the religion of the patients, thanks to several places of worship set up in the hospital.

A complete openness on the outer world and the Oregon community

In addition to these features, the St. Charles Medical Center also benefits from a specific idea of the care that it delivers to the area's inhabitants, thanks to its distance from big urban centers and its restricted field of action within the mountains of Oregon. Rather than of "inhabitants," the center speaks of "community." And just as the specialties present today within the hospital were the object of a careful census of the medical and surgical needs of this area of Oregon, it isn't possible to imagine the center being cut off from the population for which it is designed. The presence of volunteers within the hospital is a first manifestation of this will to closely associate people from the outside world with the hospital's life and its ambitious concept of care. This will is also expressed through the organizing of activities directly designed for the population of the area. Hospital management recently launched a vast cultural project together with local photographers, to explore the links between the art of photography and the field of health, through a portrayal of the various services of the hospital. A dozen regional photographers participated in the project, each working with a particular department. The local media covered the initiative, and expositions of the work are scheduled in several area cities in 2006.

Another concrete expression of this will was the creation of a foundation, as recently as 1988, to set up a regular link with the organizations, companies, and people willing to invest, or invest themselves, in the improvement of the quality of the care delivered to the community. The Foundation has thus raised $15 million since its creation, devoted to the acquisition of better know-how or technology in some specialties, but also to preventive or educational programs designed for patients and their families, and finally to the improvement of the care given to patients. Just as at its inception, the St. Charles Medical Center relies on philanthropy in all its forms—volunteering or donations, always focused on the same mission—to answer the needs of the community and healing according to its concept of care.

Prospects

Since the beginning of this century, the Bend hospital has faced a meaningful turn in its history. There has been a demographic explosion, exceptional for the area, that will change the basic data on which the previous strategic project of the establishment relied. Thus, the 220 beds of Bend, as well as the medical and surgical services, are no longer enough to welcome a population that more than doubled in the past decade. The city of Redmond itself is growing at a rate of 8% a year. The demographic projections for 2025 predict a level of population much higher than the 230,000 inhabitants today administered by Bend's hospital. Even after the modernization of the hospital and the launching of programs to achieve excellence in cardiology, orthopedics, neurosurgery, and cancer treatment, the hospital could very well be overrun yet again for lack of imagining the future, and risk asphyxia.

Thus, in 2003, the hospital management launched an ambitious enlargement and investment policy called "Expanding the Vision." A program of $128 million is called for, to build new centers in orthopedics and neurosurgery, to extend the emergency and maternity services, to finance the latest techniques and generation of products in the treatment of cancer, and to invest in an informational program for follow-up on a patient's health. For this private hospital, no public funding is possible; the project is totally financed through debt financing ($81 million), reserves ($37 million), and philanthropy ($10 million).

The St. Charles Medical Center won't loose its soul in this extension project. Outside contributions, in donations and volunteer services but also in the control exercised by the community and the local population through the Foundation, keeps the attention focused. In this context of demographic explosion and a scarcity of nurses and medical staff, the hospital relies more than ever on its own vision of care to widen the gap with other medical centers or work environments in the field of health. And because it considers that more than 80% of pathologies are directly linked to lifestyle, and the psychological mindset of the patients is directly linked to their well-being, the hospital just created a care and education center to make the population aware of the importance of these elements and to make better life choices, in the fields of nutrition, physical activity, and spiritual and psychological support.

Chapter Four

Humanitas:
The Yes Culture

HUMANITAS

Activity: Nonprofit elderly home and eldercare (6500 people in 28 residences)

Location: Rotterdam, The Netherlands

Creation: 1959

Manpower: 2400 people

In the spacious patio, illuminated by daylight, any visitor feels immediately at ease: the restaurant's tables are welcoming, the colors are bright and warm, the architecture is modern, and the ornamentation is of the best taste. The slight musical ambience coming from the bar and the burst of voices rising from a room where an activity is taking place don't let you suspect that you're in an elderly home. The only clue is the presence of a few inhabitants, some with a stroller, who come to fetch their mail or drink coffee on the patio.

The challenge to Hans Becker, president of Humanitas, was an ambitious one: to revolutionize the way of taking care of elderly people and to create a new paradigm that would become the norm in the Netherlands. The traditional support model, common to a lot of Western countries, was based on three distinct structures: elderly homes, home care, and medical establishments, where patients were often relayed by hospitals until the end of their lives. Almost half a century after the creation of an association that issued the challenge to Becker, the bet is won: Humanitas has never stopped pushing the boundaries of the traditional model.

The birth of a debate on eldercare in the Netherlands

In the sixties and seventies, the Netherlands went through an evolution, just as their European neighbors did: a lot of elderly homes were built to welcome people aged 65 and over. They featured long buildings full of inner corridors, 14-square-meter rooms, a few double rooms of 25 square meters and, as an exception, 34-square-meter flats with a bedroom and a living room for the most autonomous people. Most of these institutions also had a small living room and bathroom per story, and a huge common area for all of the residents. Health or rest homes, conceived for short stays and as a transitory step between hospital and home, are, for the most part, built on the same model.

Between the seventies and the nineties, rest and care structures follow similar trends in Europe: residences become bigger and a little more comfortable. The average size of the rooms or small flats allowed to each person stands at a little over 50 square meters. However, one aspect is neglected: residents are more and more often submitted to intensive care facilities.

Since 1988, the healthcare system for the elderly follows a different organization in the Netherlands. Traditionally, when an elderly person was living in a care residence, his/her income was poured back to social security and he/she would receive a small amount of money to cover personal expenses. Today, residents pay for their own care and stay, and retain the ability to focus their expenses on various services proposed by the residence.

A specific evolution concerns rest homes. In the sixties and seventies, rest homes were conceived for people who needed rehabilitation after hospitalization. The reason they existed was purely financial: the cost of a day at the hospital was so high that it was less expensive to go through a transition in a rest home. But the nature of these places has evolved. Today, almost 85% of the elderly stay there until the end of their life. Just like hospitals, these homes can contain several beds in each room; in such conditions, neither intimacy nor a social link is left for the elderly residents.

Psychiatric care establishments also went through important changes. The so-called mental hospitals were huge institutions, cut off from the rest of the world. They've been separated into smaller services, uniting a dozen patients each time.

Why did a debate on the care of elderly people specifically take place in the Netherlands in the nineties? Hans Becker proposes an answer: "Of all the European countries, the Netherlands has the highest percentage of people over 65 living in specialized institutions (elderly homes, medical houses, or rest homes). The arguments and wishes expressed in the course of individual discussions with elderly people or through lobbies were important. They asked for: the ability to function as autonomously and independently as possible, to have an opportunity to stay as a couple or with a member of their family, to benefit from more intimacy, to avoid having to go someplace else for specific care, to have separate spaces between living areas and care areas, to be able to maintain contact with the neighborhood and the environment, and, finally, to be offered a coherent care system."

Becker took over as the head of Humanitas at the beginning of the eldercare debate. A graduate and a teacher of economics at the University, he was recruited by the board of an association that was created in the post-war period by syndicates and social-democratic parties of the Netherlands. He was given the responsibility to restore the financial health of Humanitas, nonprofitable during the eighties, without compromising its social foundations.

The first bases of a new policy: the apartments of life

For Becker, a life as autonomous as possible in the frame of a residence had to become a possibility for a majority of patients, including the oldest or those suffering from illnesses such as Alzheimer's disease. As soon as he took up his duties, he no longer spoke of "patients" but instead referred to the residents as "clients." The needs of the elderly, expressed as clients and not as patients, was soon translated by the creation of 300 apartments of life in the Humanitas' residences in Rotterdam—three-room flats with a kitchen and a bathroom adapted to elderly people, with accessible and numerous wheelchairs and handrails and the possibility to easily set up new equipment according to needs.

But the greatest innovation brought by Humanitas wasn't those material elements. It was more the result of a slow maturation, since the creation of the association in 1959, of the principles on which a model of institution and care of the elderly should be based—principles that were reinterpreted by Becker according to the new social needs expressed. Three of these principles, highly symbolic, surpass all others. They're the leading ideas for the management of the manpower. They constitute, most of all, the three foundations of the new management model of an elderly home:

▶ The "yes culture," which meant a high level of autonomy for the elderly and that their well-being should take precedence over everything else for the staff. "It goes so far that the word 'no' has been prohibited for the Humanitas staff," comments Becker. The teams, who never seem to pay enough attention in an elderly home, have here, on the contrary, to focus all their attention on the satisfaction of an expressed need. This attitude must become a reflex—"yes" being said without thinking, without considering the cost of the request. This "yes," given *a priori*, represents a breakthrough compared to the traditional image of an elderly home. By the same logic, the staff has to make sure that the elderly people do take care of themselves. "We call that 'helping with your hands behind your back.'" It's a real challenge for the teams. "This attention given to the residents' well-being means that we have to accept that a teddy bear may be more important than a nurse, and food more important than medical care," explains Becker.

▶ The total eradication of the white smock in Humanitas establishments, not only because it refers to a past concept of the home as a medical function but also because it highlights the distance between the medical staff and the residents. Everything that has to do with medical care is carefully hidden in Humanitas residences, while activities that get people moving (like the bar, the hairdresser, and the restaurant) are shown. In the same way, anything that is likely to foster emotions and to animate interest is widely supported—demonstrations, art, animals, and even some alcohol, to follow the saying "a bottle a day keeps the doctor away."

▶ The end of the "misery islands". To keep Humanitas residences from functioning like most other establishments, it's necessary to gather various types of residents together. Healthy people live next to the unhealthy ones, the youngest keep close to the oldest, the wealthiest stay with those who have more limited resources, and people from Rotterdam gather with people from outside the city. The location of the buildings is planned to allow the Humanitas residence to become the central point of the neighborhood. Some propose a day nursery, small animals, or even a supermarket that will attract the people living in the neighborhood.

The association thus dismantles all the paradigms of a traditional elderly home: no more white smocks, but comfortable clothes for the staff, permanent attention paid to food quality, total freedom for the residents in the decoration of their flats, and a wide opening to the outer world.

The formalization of a philosophy and a new paradigm

Mere appearance? No, because behind these principles lies the philosophy and convictions of Humanitas. The well-being and the health of residents aren't only the result of a good biological functioning, but also that of a psychological, sociological, and economic well-being. If the residents are able to do things that make them proud of themselves and allow them to talk with each other or to people outside, it will reinforce their well-being and their link to the world. And everything the resident and his or her spouse are able to do need not be supervised by Humanitas, following another famous saying in the organization: "Use it or lose it."

Convinced that a way of life and sheltering are crucial to maintain this spirit, the association considers that every resident should, at a minimum, benefit from a three-room flat of at least 72 square meters, with all of the adapted facilities.

The Humanitas model could today be summed up like this:

▶ Full responsibility and autonomy for the residents. Care is strictly individual and not omnipresent. Autonomy and self-confidence are constantly stimulated. ("Give help with your hands behind your back.")

▶ Most of the care is provided by the residents themselves, with the help of volunteers. ("Too much care is worse than too little care.")

▶ A distinct separation of the living spaces and those devoted to care. The client is master in his/her own home—he/she has the right to buy his or her own apartment.

▶ No separation of couples in the residences.

▶ The fight against any institutional culture. The goal of Humanitas isn't the separation from the outside world, but, on the contrary, the reintegration of elderly people into social life.

▶ Direct communication with the neighborhood, thanks to multiple exchanges with the inhabitants, associations, and several neighborhood communities.

▶ Importation of all the elements necessary to the well-being and quality of life inside the residence—comfortable bars and restaurants, bridge clubs coming in from the outside, artistic expositions, musical activities, stamp collectors' markets, and other activities in the "village place"... it can all be found at Humanitas.

The model implies that the organization must be flexible in order to adapt to each individual and to the evolution of needs. This reactivity is made possible by the yes culture, now deeply anchored within the staff.

The results

The first 300 apartments of life were born in 1995. Today, there are more than 1000 and the number of residences more than doubled. These flats were conceived in conjunction with the association's philosophy, which is itself in harmony with the wishes of the residents. No assistance is given without a request from the residents. Even the difficult goal of welcoming the 1% of residents under constant care has been achieved. Patients suffering from Alzheimer's disease have been able to live with a maximum of independence. Everything is far from the culture of prohibition and excessive medication that can still be found in other facilities. This respect for people and for their dignity creates happiness and well-being at the end of life.

For the financial authorities, as well as for the association, this level of care and service individualization and the number of square meters given per resident could appear unaffordable at first. But more than five years of practice have shown the exact opposite: the concept developed by Humanitas is 25% less expensive than traditional approaches. Why? First of all, the rental of a three-room flat is 35% less expensive than a place in a rest home. Moreover, a lot of services are provided by family members or volunteers from the association. To keep a home and a maximum level of autonomy is less expensive than having systematic lunches or house care. And most of all, staying in a traditional residence has, in the long term, negative effects on the well-being and health of an elderly person, especially on their psychological well-being. Psychological support is rarely necessary at Humanitas, saving a lot of hours of care for the medical teams and the staff itself.

The Humanitas experiment has shown that, for the elderly, having a feeling that they're in charge of their own lives (mastering their own shelter and their own bodies), integrating a respect for intimacy and dignity, and feeling a part of a social life enhances the well-being and general good health of residents.

For the care staff, this concept of residents in charge of their own well-being and health is in complete disagreement with their education and past experiences in other institutions. At Humanitas, they're now educated to be ever-obliging, and they know that their role consists precisely in teaching the clients to do a maximum of things on their own. This new role requires flexibility on their part and everyone isn't ready to manage this yet. In fact, some studies of the Humanitas projects have shown that the elderly clients have gotten used to this new situation much faster than the association's own medical staff.

Prospects

For Humanitas, the changes are only just beginning. In the Netherlands as well as in other European countries, hospitals are becoming more and more specialized and devoted to intensive care. The association is actually concerned by this evolution, so they have started an experiment to secure less-complex hospital care inside the residences, for pathologies like diabetes, asthma, fractures, hernias, follow-up on cerebral bleeding, dialysis, and cardiac and bowel problems. This experiment also includes patients suffering from comportmental troubles, permanently confined in bed or afflicted by a disease in its terminal phase. All of this requires the latest medical techniques in the residences, dependent upon the pathologies of each patient.

The association knows that the introduction of the functions of a hospital into the apartments of life won't be easy, and the basic principles of well-being and autonomy shouldn't be forgotten. But the achievement of these new challenges is part of the yes culture, of the need for innovation and experimentation at Humanitas.

Chapter Five

ZIN: The Memory of Origins for Survival

ZIN

Activity: Seminar center, integrated in a religious community

Location: Vught, The Netherlands

Creation: 2001

The place epitomizes serenity: modern architecture, enveloped in greenery, with light-colored walls, sometimes covered in natural wood or tinted panels, furniture in a very simple design, almost bare, that invites rest, reflection, and even meditation. An ideal place to achieve some distance; ZIN is especially fit for this purpose. Nothing very original, except for the fact that this center is situated in the very heart of a religious congregation and was founded in 2001 following the express will of Brother Wim Verschuren, with the support of an experienced consultant. Today the center is managed by a company of which the community is a part.

The sole creation of this center, very open to the outside world, is in itself a little miracle, after the abrupt history of the members of the community. The congregation was indeed very close to disappearing completely in the sixties and seventies, after a long period of decline. The center exists because the Brothers discovered how to rebuild their community, recover their identity, and draw on a new wave of spirituality. They found the strength, at the beginning of a new century, to reaffirm their values and rediscover a message that was in phase with today's world.

The history of an inspired movement, swallowed by decline

The story of the congregation goes back to 1844. During the first years of the nineteenth century, the Tilburg area of the Netherlands lived in the rhythm of industrialization, with all of its consequences: an exodus of the rural population toward the cities and new centers of activity, and the growth of poverty, more accurately felt in days of crisis. Schools didn't exist. When the work stopped, people found themselves in need. Father Joannes Zwijsen, in charge of a parish in the area, was struck by the ever-growing number of the destitute population and the effects of poverty on the most vulnerable, who were mostly children. The situation reminded him of other times in history, marked by pauperism. In 1502, an anonymous Flemish painter, known as the Master of Alkmaar, was inspired by a passage of the Gospel According to St. Matthew, and created a work known as the "Seven Works of Mercy." This chapter of the Gospel notably contained the words: "Come, ye blessed of my Father, inherit the kingdom prepared for you from the foundation of the world. For I was hungry and ye gave me meat; I was thirsty and ye gave me drink; I was a stranger and ye took me in; I was naked and ye clothed me; I was sick and ye visited me; I was in prison and ye came unto me... Verily I say unto you, in as much as ye did unto one of the least of these my brethren ye have done unto me." A first movement of mercy was thus born in the sixteenth century from this message, to take care of the consequences of poverty and war.

Father Zwijsen also remembered a great French religious man, St. Vincent de Paul, also know as "the father of the poor," who dedicated his life to the most vulnerable populations. Thanks to his charisma, he convinced men and women to follow him and founded a movement solely devoted to the cause of the poorest. Their work benefited them not only in the single goal of saving their souls but also because the meeting with God comes precisely in every situation where help and assistance is given to the most destitute. In this aspect, he argued, mercy has to be efficient and materialized through facts, but effective as well.

Following this gospel message, Father Zwijsen created the Congregation of the Sisters of Charity in 1832. In 1844 he also created the "Congregation of the Brothers of Our Lady, Mother of Mercy," better known as the Brothers of Tilburg. These two religious movements paid particular attention to orphans, their instruction, and their education. The Brothers created the first schools in Tilburg, and soon expanded throughout the province of the Brabant, before establishing some schools outside the Netherlands.

The movement born from the idea of Joannes Zwijsen quickly expanded during the nineteenth and twentieth centuries, as pioneering work in the education and instruction of children. The community set up facilities in Brazil, Belgium, Indonesia, Kenya, Namibia, Surinam, and the United States. "More than 900 brothers are buried here (in Vught), brothers who implemented, in a very concrete way, the message of mercy, anonymously and with simplicity, either in the Netherlands or in other countries. They contributed to give the world a more human face. In such places, we can collect ourselves and find again the memory of our origins," tells Brother Wim Verschuren.

Wim Verschuren joined the congregation in 1963 when he was 18 years old. He was from a rural background and lost his father during World War II. He first taught in an elementary school and his first steps in the community occurred while the spiritual message of Joannes Zwijsen was falling into a deep decline. "Since the thirties, the very word of 'mercy' stopped being used in the current language. During my studies, I never heard anything about it. Or, when it was evoked, it was in a negative way, almost condescending, to outline an inequal report. The term has been further devalued because it was associated with a moral, or inspired by a moralizing will: a believer has to be merciful and obliging. The deep message and the true spirituality hidden behind this term were progressively lost," regrets Wim.

But the worse was yet to come. "In the seventies," he continues, "we lost our identity and our inspiration because of fundamental changes in the church and society. I experienced this crisis personally, as a member of our community's leadership." The post-68 revolution—political involvement, the sexual revolution, the idea that "God is dead"—produced disastrous effects, and in the Netherlands many brothers left the community. Worse, the existence of the congregation was threatened, in its very vocation and in the relevance of its message to the outside world. The dismantling of the community was well engaged. Wim himself searched for his way.

The breakthrough: finding the original inspiration and following your own path

But Wim possesses a specificity that his brothers lack. Apart from his charisma and his personal quality, he's the only one, in opposition with the congregation's principles, who studied at the University. After a few years of teaching in Vught, he studied philosophy and was immersed in the student environment of that time, and then went back to the congregation where he was welcomed into the leadership. When he returned, he benefited from an outer regard of his own community and from a perfect knowledge of the society of the sixties and seventies. Both would serve him well.

Thanks to the reflection engaged by Wim, the external impact that could have been the death of the congregation will, in fact, mark its spiritual resurrection and the rebirth of a real movement. "We could only overcome this crisis by renewing with our original spirituality and starting a process of re-creation. The first question we asked was: what can make man happy? In the course of this questioning, we rediscovered mercy and we understood that it was at the heart of everything. That is what got us on the move again." Yet, just as St. Vincent de Paul did in his time, the concept of mercy had to be adapted to the current context.

After observing the congregation, Wim started from a simple fact: "The brothers had learned how to behave mercifully with others but not with themselves. This point was absolutely dramatic! How would we develop self-esteem in our own community? How would we step from the word to true mercy?" Another fact showed him the contradiction with today's society. Traditionally, the hierarchy of the congregation used to send their orders through letters that were then read to the whole brotherhood. Some brothers would learn in this way that they were to be sent abroad to join one of the foreign congregations. This management, based on authority and discipline, still vivid in the seventies, deeply disturbed Wim.

But how would he recreate a new state of mind, a new identity? The method engaged by Wim aimed to plunge again into a process of spiritual reflection. The first step was an invitation to observation and meditation, with meditation being recognized as a method and a way of looking at the world. The second step was to follow one's heart. Then, and only then, could they act or make a decision. "Mercy is tenderness and strength, action and contemplation at the same time," sums up Wim. "Only by giving mercy back its spiritual dimension could it become a guideline for us again and give us the vision of what our community could do for this world to become better."

This spiritual reflection didn't happen in a few days. "It took us several years to recover our new identity," admits Wim. "It became a daily guideline for us, to conduct our works and to orient our way of leading the community." No more elections to assign the head of the congregation. Instead they established relations based on trust and listening, for all the members to follow the same route. After the last day's prayer, the Brothers share a moment of conviviality, gathered around a glass of wine. And although poverty and chastity vows are still respected, the Brothers are far from cut off from the world. Their rooms are now furnished with televisions. In the same way, they live next to outside visitors who come to work or step aside for a while at the ZIN Center. Yet, they don't forget their roots; the memory of the brothers buried in Vught is evoked on their birthdays. At a time when other brotherhoods hardly survive, the movement inspired by Joannes Zwijsen lives again and develops itself in a new way, adapted to the actual society.

A resurrection: The movement of mercy

As a matter of fact, the spiritual revolution at work among the Brothers of Tilburg is strongly mirrored in society: "At the end of the twentieth century, the interest is such that we can talk of a new movement of mercy in our country and anywhere else in the world." The movement of mercy really started in 1988 in the Netherlands. A campaign of recruitment of new members for the community was launched, through the press and advertisement. Not only did the campaign go further than hoped but it also raised the interest of the population. To answer the demand, the congregation instated the possibility to become an "associate to the movement of mercy." Since then, several thousand members and sympathizers gather together during regional or national meetings.

"Guessing why mercy has become attractive again today is an interesting question," wonders Wim. "A few reasons can be given. First of all, we interpret and experience mercy as a fundamental attitude, essential for us as human beings. That's why we speak of a spirituality of mercy. And acts of mercy derive from it. Thus, to become a merciful man or woman is part of a personal development process: we all have to follow our path to achieve this goal. Mercy is our destination."

"The second reason: the rediscovery of the second commandment, 'love thy neighbor as you love yourself,' in all its meaning. Generations of wealthy people undertook the seven acts of mercy, with devotion, sometimes night and day. But they were not invited to love themselves and to be merciful with themselves. This ascetic life could have terrible consequences. Because they fought to work hard, they were also harsh with themselves and in their relationship to others. In our discussions, this was a recurring theme. Mercy is all about paying attention to the other's weaknesses but also to one's self."

"The field of application of mercy is moreover unlimited and has to appear in each and every relationship we have. Not only when someone is in need, but also between a man and a woman, between parents and children, in work, in sports, etc. I meet a lot of people every day, and personally, those teachings helped me on a daily basis to live in the ways of mercy."

"This is why," adds Wim, "all the aspects of mercy touch a lot of people nowadays. They bring answers to essential questions: what gives sense to life and makes it worthwhile? How to treat distress and suffering? This is an answer to the paralyzing feeling of failure and the constant impression of being unable to reach their goals that most people feel both in their personal and professional life. Just as it meets their wish of a simple life, closer to their true aspirations. Thus the term of mercy has returned. You can hear it on television, sometimes associated with the word of compassion."

Did Wim anticipate the echo his own reflection would get when he initiated the movement of spiritual renewal of the congregation? Certainly not. "Our community had to go through a deep crisis before we were able to find again the true meaning of mercy."

In retrospect, what were the main factors of success, according to Wim? "A shared vision, intuition, the courage to take risks, even to disobey orders that came from another age. The ability, also, to mobilize, by asking everyone to make one step ahead of what he had expected. And finally, the will to go forward, while changing our route when needed." Wim, as the superior of the congregation, had to make some difficult decisions, including putting an end to some missions abroad, even in countries that needed the congregation's presence. But the very existence of the community was at stake. In the same manner, he didn't hesitate to sell the publishing house of scholarly and educational books, to create the company that would sustain the new seminar activity and make important investment in Vught. ZIN is today a splendid place for hosting seminars, but also for holding thematic meetings or artistic activities. In fact, in Great Britain, another congregation is interested in creating such a place.

Prospects

For Wim Verschuren, the movement isn't circumscribed within the borders of the congregation, nor supported by the sole successors of the Brothers of Tilburg. It is constantly enriched by other sources, notably the contributions of other religions. This spiritual dimension is now supported by other large movements. "Which isn't surprising," remarks Wim, "since the true meaning of mercy is love." In his opinion, philosophical streams, such as those of Levinas, contributed to re-establish the true meaning of mercy in the world. And famous world-class figures, like Mother Theresa, Nelson Mandela, and the Dalai Lama, embody it.

A dynamic was born, represented in the Netherlands today in the fields of health, education, and politics. "Mercy unites people," adds Wim. "We can testify to that, through the center we created in 2001, which is mainly designed for leaders. What does mercy mean for a manager, a company, or the world? This movement brings life and generates hope. I think that it is today the only way to go toward a peaceful world. Peace is the most precious gift of mercy," concludes Wim.

Leading Organizational Transformation in a Rapidly Changing World

Shoji Shiba
and
David Walden

INTRODUCTION TO SECTION 2

For many years, we, particularly Shoji Shiba, have been investigating management of breakthrough [Shiba98, Walden93]. Shoji Shiba has observed and run workshops on breakthrough management throughout the world. Our 2001 book, *Four Practical Revolutions in Management* [Shiba01], included two chapters on breakthrough management.

In 2003, Shoji Shiba published a complete book, titled *Breakthrough Management*, in Japanese [Shiba03]. That book was well received in Japan and won the 2004 Nikkei Quality Management Literature Award for which it was nominated by the Deming Committee.

The following five chapters are a major revision and update of about half of Shoji Shiba's 2003 book. In addition to the obvious change of being in English rather than Japanese, these chapters include more examples from countries other than Japan and some new concepts. The first two chapters introduce the importance of breakthrough in today's rapidly changing, globalized world. The next three chapters discuss eight principles for leading organizational transformation.

We are currently working on a follow-on book that also updates the other half of Shoji Shiba's 2003 book. For information about its contents and how to obtain a copy, see:

www.walden-family.com/breakthrough

Chapter Six

Rapid Change in a Global World

We are in an age of enormous change—great change has happened and is happening. While there is significant change in the U.S. and in Europe, the most dramatic changes are happening in Asia, particularly in China and India. These changes impact the whole world. They may threaten the position of the United States in the rest of the world.

Change can be a source of opportunity. It can also threaten survival. If your business involves commodity products—products that can be replicated elsewhere in the world—the question you face is how to find the opportunity in change and thus survive.

6.1 Change from China

Mr. S. Okuda is chairman of Toyota. He also is chairman of Keidan-Ren, the most powerful organization of CEOs in Japan. On November 11, 2003, Mr. Okuda, in his capacity of chairman of Keidan-Ren, gave a presentation to a number of top Japanese businesspeople, executives, and managers. In his presentation he noted:

> China has become the world's top producer of steel, small-sized motors, and home electrical appliances such as refrigerators.

Fast development in these areas has been a result of two important factors:

⬤ Foreign investment in China

⬤ The high quality of the Chinese workforce

The quality of the workforce in China is superb. As an example, suppose you needed ten workers and listed the following qualifications in your advertisement:

⬤ 20–24 years of age

⬤ Right handed

⬤ Eyesight better than 2.0 [20/20]

⬤ Height 155–165 cm

You would surely have 100 qualified applicants the following day. In addition, those people would be eager to work overtime as well as Saturdays and Sundays. Their wages would be about one-twentieth that of similar workers in Japan.

Japan cannot compete with China in the production of like products. China has an enormous competitive advantage in its quality of workforce. We must clearly understand that competition is not possible in the field of "commoditized" products.

What do we do, then, for future survival?

What Mr. Okuda said about Japan's difficulty in competing with China is true for the rest of the world as well. Labor used to be cheap in Hungary, Ireland, Spain, etc., but these countries now have difficulty competing with the labor available in China. And, of course, labor in the U.S. has not been cheap for many years.

China also is driving out the competition in other countries' home markets. Four years ago there was a manufacturing company in Budapest, Hungary, that made train equipment, but the company went bankrupt. In October 2004, Shoji Shiba visited and photographed the Személybe Járar (Four Tigers Market) that now exists in the train factory location (see Figure 6-1). The manufacturing environment is still intact, for instance, large industrial cranes on tracks run along the ceiling (see Figure 6-2); but by 2004 the factory buildings were home to rooms full of clothes, lingerie, and toys imported from China. Street stalls located between the buildings sold casual clothes and shoes out of shipping containers that opened into retail sales spaces. Hungarian industry cannot compete with these products.

Interestingly, the people working in the Four Tigers Market are largely Chinese, not Hungarian. We are not sure how they come to be in Hungary.

The manual labor workforce is not China's only excellent workforce. The workforce of Chinese knowledge workers is also developing, to the point where many Japanese companies are outsourcing software work to China, and Microsoft's research center in China has been described in the U.S. business press. Soon, it may be hard to compete with China in the area of knowledge work as well as manual work.

More than that, the Chinese are developing excellent management skills. Since China opened itself to participation in the World Trade Organization (WTO), globalization has become a primary task of Chinese managers. China wants to become the "plant for the world." The December 24, 2004, issue of *The New York Times* had an article ("In Roaring China, Sweaters Are West of Socks City," pp. A1 & C3) describing how the city of Datang, China, specializes in manufacturing socks—9 billion pairs of socks a year. The article says that to the west of Socks City is Sweater City and Kid's Clothing City. To the south …is Underwear City.

Figure 6-1. Top: Old factory from outside; Bottom: Reused building—The Four Tigers Market

Figure 6-2. Reuse of a train factory

China is promoting the management training required for globalization—"globalization management training"—on three fronts:

1. Joint ventures with foreign firms

2. Government Department of Labor qualifying examinations for managers

3. Diffusion of MBA programs

Joint ventures with China have been frequently documented in the business press, at least in the U.S.

China has a *long* history of qualifying for higher positions by way of examinations. Thus, it is quite natural for China to establish qualifying examinations as a component in promoting the management training required for globalization. There are three grades of examinations. The grade 3 examination qualifies a person to be a middle manager. Grade 2 relates to being a vice president. Grade 1 is to be a CEO or COO. The grade 3 and grade 2 training and examination systems have been operating since 2002. In parallel with setting up qualifications and examinations for three levels of management skill, the Chinese government has established training mechanisms for the examinations. The grade 1 system began operating in 2004 with an 18-week, 2 days-a-week course.[1]

Beijing University is offering an International MBA. Its promotional literature says, "If you want to be a CEO in the new century, this school is a 'West Point' for management." The teaching is done in English, often in weekend sessions that students can fit in with their existing jobs. Such international MBA programs are happening at other prestigious universities, for instance, Chinhua University in Beijing, Fudan University in Shanghai, and Lingnun University in Gan Zu. Some of these programs have alliances with foreign universities, for instance with the MIT Sloan School of Management.

In China, management education, particularly an MBA, has become a qualification to become a manager. In another break with the past, people are becoming senior managers at younger ages, particularly when they have an MBA. For instance, in 2001 in the management team of the company Suzhou, the president was 37 years old and had an MBA, the plant manager was 40 with an MBA, the sales director was 44 with a BA, the marketing manager was 38 with a BA, the IT manager was 37 with a BA, the quality manager was 32 with a BA, the financial manager had an MBA, and the logistics manager was 40 with a BA. In the past, long seniority, possibly based on a rise from the factory floor, might have been more common in Chinese companies.

Also, in at least one instance, a Chinese company purchased a U.S. business partly as a way of getting more management talent. In late 2004, IBM announced the sale of its personal computer business to the Chinese company Lenovo. An article in the December 28, 2004, issue of *The New York Times*[2] suggested that at least part of the reason for this purchase by Lenovo was to acquire IBM's experienced management team that came with the personal computer business.

These rapid changes are perceived within China as well as outside. In 2002, 2003, and 2004, Shoji Shiba asked his students in the International MBA program at Fudan University about changes in Shanghai. Each year he asked the students to rank the areas of greatest change in Shanghai. Table 6-1 summarizes how the students responded.

As shown in the table, the area of greatest change moved in three years from infrastructure to globalization to social life—very big change over a very short period.

By *infrastructure*, the students meant: buildings; highways, subways, and bridges; environment (water, green space, etc.); population inflow; income and gross domestic product. By *globalization*, the students meant: foreign companies (joint ventures, branch offices, investment, etc.); foreigners (businesspeople, foreign students, etc.); worldwide events; language schools. Change in *social life* was described in less tangible terms by the students than were infrastructure and globalization. Social life changes included:

- New styles of consumption—new consumer goods (cars, clothing, etc.), more opportunities for consumption

- New social trends—new mentalities (e.g., divorce), demographic changes (increasing numbers of people coming to Shanghai from the country and the reverse)[3]

- Unfavorable effects (layoffs by some companies as China's planned economy ended), congestion (e.g., cars), rising costs (housing, etc.), etc.

Table 6-1. *Perception of Fudan University I-MBA students of recent change in Shanghai*

	2002	2003	2004
Infrastructure	53.8%	38.8%	38.6%
Globalization	20.0%	41.8%	9.1%
Social life	25.4%	19.4%	52.3%
Number of students	67	67	44

In addition to providing severe competition to businesses throughout the world, China will have a big impact as a market itself. For instance, an article on page 35 of the July 12, 2004, issue of *Nikkei Business* forecasts the change in the worldwide car market between 2003 and 2020. The markets in the U.S. and Europe do not grow expansively—they are saturated. However, the number of cars produced for the domestic market in China goes from 439×10^4 to 1700×10^4. The same is likely to happen for other types of products.

Yet, the change in China is such that even Chinese companies are sometimes struggling to compete. On December 25, 2005, at a training seminar of the Shanghai CQM for the grade 1 qualifying examination (more about this below), Shoji Shiba worked with executives such as chief executive officers, chief operating officers, vice presidents, and directors of large- and medium-scaled companies in the Shanghai area and asked them, "What is the biggest change in your business in 2005?" There were many answers, but they could be boiled down into a few categories:

- The cost of labor and materials increased.[4]

- The exchange rate had a big effect.

- Competition became harder and harder.

- The price for the product went down.

- The export market increased [a good thing].

In response to the follow-on question, "What did you do about it?", the answers were of the form:

- Move the factory away from Shanghai to where land and labor is cheaper.

- Try a new product mix.

- Restructure the company.

- Improve quality.

- Change the mentality of management.

In response to a further follow-on question about results, it became clear some companies did better in 2005 and some did worse. In Shoji Shiba's small sample, six companies reported increased sales while three reported decreased sales. Two reported a profit increase, and four reported a profit decrease. A couple reported opening new markets.

In general, the change over the past two years has been enormous. Some things that were true two years ago are no longer true. For instance, Figure 6-3 shows the change over the past couple of years in what countries' cars are selling in the internal automobile market in China.[5] Also, almost all automobiles or automobile parts sold in China are now made in China, although in many cases in Chinese company joint ventures with foreign companies; furthermore, the Chinese companies are also increasingly producing automobiles themselves with technology and know-how obtained from their foreign partners.[6]

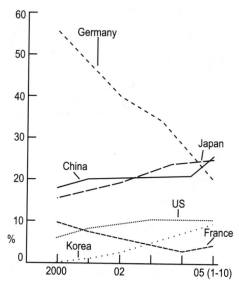

Figure 6-3. China automobile market by country

Shoji Shiba, who travels the world studying and teaching business, has never seen a country change so fast—much faster than the changes he saw in Japan in the 1960s and 1970s. It seems inevitable that the changes in China will continue to jar the rest of the world for years to come.

6.2 Change from India

Another major place of change and source of change in the rest of the world is India. If China wants to become the "plant of the world," India seems on its way to becoming the "back office of the world."

In particular, India is trying to become a major software center for the world. As shown in Figure 6-4,[7] between 1995 and 2003, the value of export software work taken in by India rose from $.7 billion to $15 billion. Over the last four years of this period, the value doubled.

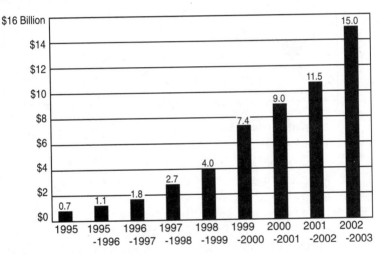

Figure 6-4. IT *export work taken in by India*

Figure 6-5 shows why India is becoming a top-notch competitor in the software area. The vertical axis is a measure of the "goodness" of human resources in a country's software industry—a combination of the number of engineers, their skill, and their cost. The horizontal axis is the number of highly qualified vendors of software. For our purposes here, the noteworthy aspect of this figure is that India has nearly caught up with the U.K., U.S., and Japan in terms of the overall quality (capacity, skill, and cost) of their software industry.

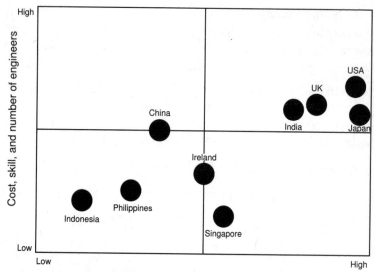

Figure 6-5. IT positioning

A second strength of India in the changing world is in manufacturing. In 1988, the Confederation of Indian Industry (CII) set up a TQM division and began the intensive diffusion of quality methods. The level of quality of Indian industry has been such that between 1995 and 2005 ninety-five Indian companies have been TPM Award Winners, and sixteen Indian companies had won the Deming Prize and Japan Quality Medal. In the U.S. only two companies have ever won the Deming Prize (Florida Power and Light in 1989 and ATT Power Systems in 1994). In Taiwan, only one company had ever won the Deming Prize (Phillips in 1991).

Of course, companies in only a few countries even bother to challenge the Deming Prize, which begs the question of why have so many Indian companies successfully challenged the prize. The answer is that Indian companies are competing to be excellent; applying for the prize provides both a target for improvement and benefits a company's reputation. (That eight companies in Thailand have won the Deming Prize since 2001 may be indicative of another coming Asian competitive powerhouse.)

In a slightly different domain, at the International Conference on Quality Circles in Bangkok in December 2004, there were more participants from India than from any other country except Thailand. The QC Circle activity in India today is like it was in Japan in the 1970s.

Another important component of India's drive for and success in improved quality across its manufacturing activities is its embracing the methods of cross-company mutual learning.

Shoji Shiba was able to get a high-level view of India's industrial strategy on July 25, 2004, when he was invited to meet for an hour with Dr. A.P.J. Abdul Kalam, the president of India. Dr. Kalam told Shoji Shiba that India has three types of companies:

- Companies with an R&D capability to create unique technologies
- Companies that license technology and do some design
- Companies that do manufacturing according to a specification given to them

The issue in each case is how to push that type of company to a higher level.

The way Shoji Shiba's meeting with President Kalam came about brought home to Shoji Shiba the insight that one of the skills of great leaders is quick action at cutting through bureaucracy. Shoji Shiba was in New Delhi for three weeks giving a seminar. A seminar participant who was well connected in the government passed along to the president's office information about what Shoji Shiba was teaching. Immediately an invitation came to visit the president.

A similar thing had happened in Hungary in 1989 when Shoji Shiba was giving a seminar in Budapest, and the Hungarian Minister of Industry, L. Kapoli, invited Shoji Shiba to come directly to his office.

And, in the U.S., in late 1990, the term of Shoji Shiba's secondment from Tsukuba University to MIT had expired. When U.S. Secretary of Commerce Robert A. Mosbacher heard that Shoji Shiba had to return to Japan, he immediately wrote to the Japanese Ambassador to the U.S. asking that Shoji Shiba be allowed to stay in the U.S. helping U.S. industry for an additional period of time.

6.3 Change in the U.S. and Europe

Even though the competition is strong, the U.S. has not been standing still. Since 1990, Shoji Shiba has been regularly visiting U.S. companies.[8] In 1990, no U.S. company Shoji Shiba saw practiced all of the elements of a world-class factory.[9] By 1998–9, the best U.S. companies, including Intel, HP, Honeywell, and General Motors, had all of the elements of a world-class factory.

Another example comes from Shoji Shiba's students in MIT's Leaders for Manufacturing (LFM) program. The LFM students are highly qualified for graduate school and typically have several years of industrial or business experience before attending the program. In 2002, Shoji Shiba asked the LFM students to participate in an informal survey of their awareness of quality methods that are common to world-class factories.

As shown in Figure 6-6, on average half of the students did not know or had not heard of the various quality methods. However, the other half of the students did know of the methods, and a majority of those students had personally used or taught the methods. This is a significant change from our impression of our LFM students' awareness of such methods five and ten years before. Shoji Shiba also believes that you would not find such a high level of awareness in any other country. (Even in Japan the level of awareness is a bit less than it once was.)

		Do not know/Have not heard of	Know	Personally Used	Taught
Improvement Steps (7 steps, etc.)		57%	18%	25%	
7 Tools					
	Pareto				
	Cause and Effect	32	27	41	
	Checklist				
	Control Chart				
Affinity					
Tree Diagram					
5S		43	30	27	
Visual Factory		68	14	18	
Six Sigma					
Benchmarking					
Concept Engineering					
SPC					
Taguchi		58	40		3
Experimental Design					

Figure 6-6. *Student skill evaluation*

Historically, the U.S. has been strong in strategy but weaker in operations than other countries. However, over the past 15 years, the U.S. has also achieved great strength in operations. For instance, the Boeing 737 "moving line" production system for its 737 airplane includes standardization, just-in-time, etc.—all of the elements of a world-class factory. Curiously, having a strong operations capability facilitates globalization; without it, it is difficult to set up reliable factories outside the U.S.

Over the same time period Japan has developed a decent capability in strategy but has lost some capability in operations (with some notable exceptions such as Toyota). Japan's loss of operations capability results from a shortage of manpower, top management refocusing its attention on strategy, and a deemphasis on quality improvement training.

———

Even universities are pushing for breakthrough. The Massachusetts Institute of Technology, with which we both have been affiliated on and off over the years, has recently made a symbolic gesture toward breakthrough. One of the science buildings at MIT (top of Figure 6-7) looks like it stood for efficiency; it houses the chemistry department. The new Ray and Maria Stata Center building (bottom of the figure) clearly stands for something beyond efficiency. (It houses the electrical engineering and computer science department, among other things.) MIT President Charles Vest said:

> MIT needed to be as bold at the start of twenty-first century as our predecessors had been at the start of the twentieth century. The time had come to build a facility, the physical form of which signaled the intellectual brashness, energy, and excellence held within. This building must display our soul as well as contain it.

———

Europe also has not been standing still. While its impact on the world's economies and businesses may not be as great as the changes coming from China and India, some of the most "advanced" ways of thinking about business are happening in Europe. We will introduce several case studies of European companies in Chapters 8–10.

Figure 6-7. Top: Dreyfus Building, I.M. Pei architect, built 1967–70; Bottom: Ray and Maria Stata Center, Frank Gehry architect, opened May 7, 2004

Notes

1. Shoji Shiba was the first speaker for two days (December 14–15, 2003) at the inaugural grade 1 course.

2. "Outsourcing to the U.S.," David Barboza, pp. C1–C2.

3. The Chinese are also creating and moving to the suburbs, according to an article in a China Air flight magazine in about September 2004. Yosemite Villa and Venice Water Townhouses are housing developments built around (probably man-made) lakes distant from the center of Shanghai. The creation of suburbs requires cars, which in turn will move China further into the international competition for available oil. These suburban homes are being furnished with modern furniture.

4. In late 2005, Shoji Shiba heard that the one-year increase in minimum wages in the nine cities of Shanghai, Shencheng, Guangzhou, Suzhou, Amoi, Tenjin, Beijing, Chintao, and Dalian averaged an increase of 17%, with the minimum increase of 6.4% in Beijing and the maximum increase of 34.1% in Guangzhou.

5. *Nikkei* newspaper, December 8, 2005.

6. "Thanks to Detroit, China is Poised to Lead," *The New York Times*, March 12, 2003, section 3, pp. 1&9.

7. Derived from *Fole*, October 2004, p. 5.

8. As part of the annual two-week factory tour of the graduate students in MIT's Leaders for Manufacturing (LFM) program.

9. Czarnecki, H., Schroer, B., Adams, M., and Spann, M., 2000: "Continuous Process Improvement When It Counts Most," *Quality Progress*, May, p. 78.

Chapter Seven

Exploiting the 10X Change

In this chapter we discuss the nature of change in today's world. In particular, we discuss exploiting the 10X change by managing breakthrough.

7.1 10X change

In his book *Only the Paranoid Survive*,[1] Andy Grove illustrated great insight about change in our time. He starts by paraphrasing five forces that Michael Porter said determine the competitive well-being of a business (which we paraphrase still further):

▶ The strength of a company's current competitors

▶ The strength of a company's suppliers

▶ The strength of a company's customers

▶ The strength of a company's potential competitors

▶ The possibility the company's product can be built or delivered in a different way

To this list Grove adds a sixth element:

▶ The company's situation with regard to other companies whose businesses complement the company's business

Grove shows these forces in what he calls a Six Forces Diagram, as shown in Figure 7-1.

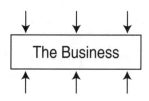

Figure 7-1. Grove's Six Forces Diagram

The six forces can be sufficient to deal with normal business pressures. However, suppose one of the six forces is suddenly increased by a factor of ten, as illustrated in Figure 7-2. For instance, suppose a competitor offers the equivalent of your product at one-tenth the price and perhaps more capability; this is a 10X change. When a 10X change happens, says Grove, a business gets really hard to manage. You lose control of your business. Eventually, the industry will settle down with the new paradigm, and your company may or may not be one of the survivors. Unfortunately, a company often does not or cannot anticipate when a 10X change is about to happen.

In his book, Grove described the instance of transition shown in Figure 7-2 as an inflection point in what he called the inflection curve (see Figure 7-3).

As we look at Figure 7-3 and reflect on the prior two eras of change and management (control from the 1930s and 1940s and incremental improvement from the 1970s and 1980s), we understand that a new era has begun—the era of breakthrough that had started in the mid-1990s as was so well formulated in Grove's book as being the result of 10X changes. Control and incremental improvement are no longer sufficient in the face of a 10X change; something dramatic has to be done to counteract the decline of the old business in the face of the 10X change. (Even if the current business appears to be losing ground very slowly, as shown by curve A', it will likely eventually disappear.) To counteract the decline of the existing business, the company needs to fundamentally change its business—switch from path A or A' to path B in Figure 7-3.

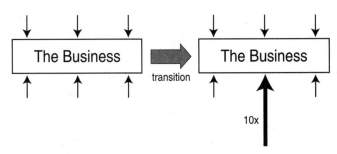

Figure 7-2. A 10X *transition*

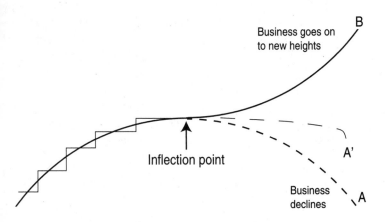

Figure 7-3. *The inflection curve*

There are many reasons why a business may begin to decline and a new business must be sought. Traditionally, products have a life cycle and must be replaced periodically by upgraded products; or markets may become saturated and, thus, no longer provide the growth opportunity that investors expect. However, a 10X change is bigger or more sudden than those more-usual problems and may come from sources such as a) rapid or dramatic price decreases, b) dramatic market changes, or c) societal incidents. They may also simply come from d) a clear insight or understanding that a value shift has happened, which could be a result of a, b, or c.

An example of *dramatic price decrease* has been seen over the history of the computer industry. The computer industry has seen a series of A-to-B changes: from the mainframe computers oriented primarily to IT departments, to mini-computers with a different set of customers particularly in the process control area, to workstations as desktop computers for engineers, to personal computers initially for businesspeople on their desktops and eventually for everyone on their desktops, to users at their desktop computers getting much of their computational and information retrieval power through interactions across the Internet. Each of these changes has come about because the technology for making computers made it possible to provide more powerful computers at dramatically less-expensive prices. Also, arguably, each step in the change of the computer business took advantage of the desire for another department or function of business to escape from more-centralized control of its computer operations; thus, another component of the continuing changes in the computer industry has been a *latent dramatic market change*.

The sale by IBM of its personal computer business to the Chinese company Lenovo is perhaps the most recent major result of the continuing dramatic price decreases in the computer industry. IBM is apparently increasingly moving to selling services and was no longer satisfied with the money it could make in the personal computer business.

Another example in the price area is the rapid decrease in the retail price of DVD recorders in Japan, which has dropped as shown in Table 7-1.[2]

Table 7-1. DVD *recorder price decreases*

Year	Price	Percent
2000	100	
2001	53	47
2002	37	21
2003	26	30
2004	19	23
2005	15	21

An example *dramatic market change* comes from a Japanese construction company that built industrial plants in the 1970s (as pictured in the top part of Figure 7-4), moved to building city skyscrapers in the 1980s (bottom part of Figure 7-4) that were then needed by society, and then moved in the 1990s to building "leisure structures" such as large stadiums (Figure 7-5).

We will study another example of repeated dramatic market changes in the case study of FAVI that is presented in section 9.2; you might glance at Figure 9-1 now.

The Shanghai Toothpaste Company provides an example of a company facing a 10X change from a *societal incident*. Many companies in China were privatized as China adopted non-Communistic market practices in recent years—privatization was a 10X change for these traditionally government-owned companies because they could no longer expect government support and markets. Some survived the change and some did not. The Shanghai Toothpaste Company's original business was manufacturing toothpaste for the domestic market, which, in time, expanded to include the export of the tooth-

Figure 7-4. Japanese construction company's changing businesses: top, 1970s; bottom, 1980s

paste it made. Then they were struck with the 10X change of privatization and the need for an A-to-B change in the business. As shown in the top part of Figure 7-6, Shanghai Toothpaste moved into the business of selling compounds that went into toothpaste and machines to fill toothpaste tubes and print the labels. They encouraged other, new companies to go into

Figure 7-5. *Japanese construction company's changing businesses: 1990s*

the toothpaste manufacturing and sales business (i.e., Shanghai Toothpaste created competitors for its original business), and Shanghai Toothpaste supplied these companies. In some sense they moved from being only a manufacturing company to being a manufacturing and engineering company. Starting in about 2000, the company has moved its business again—to providing mouth-related services in chain stores. The company hires dentists and dental hygienists and situates them in retail locations. The top part of the figure is a diagram for illustrative purposes only and does not accurately portray either the time axis or the results axis (we didn't have this detailed information available to us); the bottom part of the

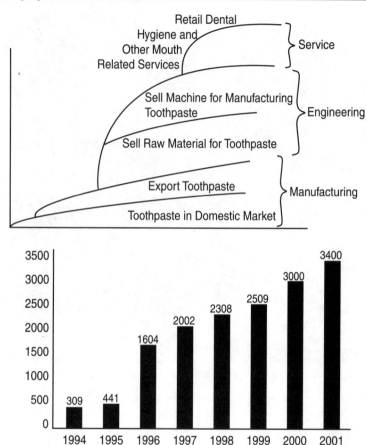

Figure 7-6. *Changes at Shanghai Toothpaste Company*

figure shows actual profit figures for the listed period of time. (The units of the profit axis are 10,000s of Chinese RMBs.)

The 10X change, for example from societal incidents, can be bigger than an industry or a collection of competitors. For instance, September 11, 2001, caused various 10X changes for the U.S. (e.g., expansion of anything related to "antiterrorism") and for some other countries. For at least a period of time, the 2003 SARS epidemic caused a 10X change—China-based elements in supply chains simply stopped. China's joining the World Trade Organization resulted in a 10X change in management thinking in China, which in turn is having a 10X change on the global economy. It is beginning to appear that the European Union's change in currency to the euro is resulting in a 10X change, i.e., in European standards and in competitiveness to the dollar.

It also works the other way. For instance, the integrated circuit certainly resulted in various 10X changes, some of which might be called societal incidents. The Internet has had similar effects.

Perhaps other examples of such A-to-B changes in business will come to mind for readers.

The columns of Figure 7-7 show our assessments of the types of 10X changes (listed a few pages ago) that were seen by the companies we describe in this book. The rows of the figure relate to the three ways to create a new business as discussed in section 7.2. Earlier in this section we discussed points b, c, and d within Figure 7-7.

7.2 Three ways to create a new business

Typically, creation of a new business happens in one of three ways:

▶ Technology based

▶ Supply chain based

▶ Customer based

In the last section we mentioned several of a succession of changes that were customer-based—the Shanghai Toothpaste Company, the Japanese construction company, and FAVI.

Source of potential or sudden weakness in the market

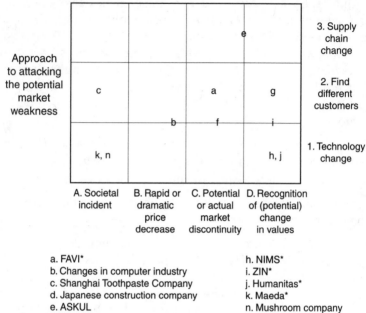

Figure 7-7. *Market weaknesses and ways of attack*

In the rest of this section, we will give specific examples of changes that were supply-chain-driven (ASKUL) and technology-driven (Okamoto Glass). The changes in the computer industry were also technology-based, but in that case no single company was able to make the successive leap from A to B; it was always a new company that made the A-to-B leap.

ASKUL—Supply-chain-based change

For years the Japanese stationery and office supplies market was monopolized by the large company KOKUYO. In this environment, a small company promoting new products had little chance. In this environment, ASKUL was started, to address the desire of the parent company, PLUS, to get a bigger foothold in the market dominated by KOKUYO. From its first sale in 1994, the company grew to be a successful venture by 1999 and has continued growing since.[3]

The essence of the business concept of ASKUL (point e in Figure 7-7) was to change the supply chain in the stationery industry. ASKUL recognized that the market was ripe for a change and the potential for expanded use of advanced IT technology existed.

A "blue sky committee" investigated the future direction of a new business, defining the ideal customers and the ideal distribution system. They concluded they should not distribute to dealers or retail shows, channels that KOKUYO dominated, but rather should go directly to customers. They also decided they should avoid big and medium-sized companies demanding full service traditionally provided by customer service organizations in dealers and large retail shops. Rather, they focused on small companies that until then had to buy their office supplies in retail shops.

In 1992, Mr. S. Iwata (of the PLUS company) spun out with a two-person team and started the ASKUL venture. "ASKUL" meant "deliver tomorrow." Mr. Iwata believed that *time* could create new additional value. ASKUL offered next-day delivery of orders made by phone, fax, or the Internet from a 6,000-item catalog. Next-day delivery rate was 99.7 percent, with same-day delivery for orders placed by 11 a.m. to locations within Tokyo and Osaka. Forty-percent discounts from list price were offered to all customers.

As shown in Figure 7-8, they created a virtual company with a minimal central ASKUL staff; a majority of the business functions were handled by out-source affiliates, temporary workers, and part-time workers. Reporting to the president of ASKUL were the financial and project innovation departments along with the organizations that handled their key business processes: customer support, efficient customer response, business planning, and back office. The ASKUL employees served in one of three roles: staff handling the core daily jobs, innovators improving the current business, and entrepreneurs looking five years into the future.

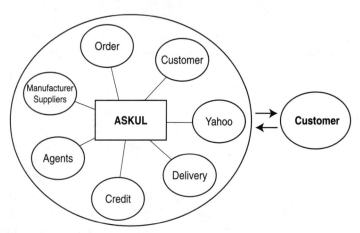

Figure 7-8. ASKUL virtual company

Rather than only offering products made by PLUS, ASKUL concluded that its real business purpose was to deliver all products regardless of manufacturer. Offering a forty-percent discount from list to all their customers drew criticism and resistance from the traditional stationery industry. However, ASKUL refused to compromise—its business purpose was to create the optimum system from a societal point of view. ASKUL concluded its job was not to sell office suppies but to create a system for how to sell office supplies. Using information technology, ASKUL made each day's orders immediately visible and undertook daily intensive analysis to enable quick action on new strategies or tactics with items and prices. The company worked jointly on this with suppliers and manufacturers (including those not traditionally part of the office supply industry). Such analysis and collaboration resulted in delivery of food and drink, foot warmers, etc., along with office supplies.

ASKUL's initial supply-chain-based attempt to attack the Japanese stationery market was motivated by the parent company's desire to gain a bigger foothold in the market. The blue sky committee that launched the particular mode of attack apparently recognized the possibility of instigating a 10X change in the market via changes in the supply chain.

Figure 7-9 shows ASKUL's sales from its inception through 2004. The sales of the last several years have begun to hint at market saturation; thus, ASKUL has put out a new catalog for the healthcare rather than stationery business. It is trying to make a customer-based change that still utilizes its supply chain innovations.

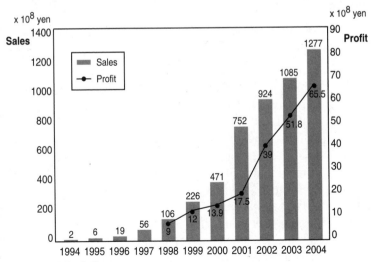

Figure 7-9. ASKUL *sales history*

Okamoto Glass—Technology-based change

Okamoto Glass (point f in Figure 7-7) has stuck with glass-making technology and advances in that technology, but they recognized that such technologies would lead it into different markets.

Okamoto Glass has existed since 1928. Originally its business was manufacturing cut glass for the consumer market. In 1977, the company moved into industrial glass production. By 1980 the company's industrial glass products included (on the one hand) automobile "hard lenses," airplane windshield glass, electrical range (and microwave door) glass, and (on the other hand) special illumination for supermarkets (to make meat look pretty).

The expansion into industrial glass products continued. For instance, by 1996, the company was making reflectors for projectors where the glass needs to be durable to withstand high temperatures. This required technology for casting and cutting delicate glass pieces. Also by 1996, the company was making dental light mirrors. One can see how each of these was an extrapolation on the 1980 products.

Behind this dramatic business change was a lot of research and development—toward high-function glass, lenses, and filtering of light.

In another technology-based example from China, the Shanghai Pudong Tiencu Mushroom Co. Ltd. wanted continued business growth, but it was difficult and too expensive to expand the amount of land they had in the Shanghai region. (Also, in general, there are restrictions on people moving in China.) Thus, the company made a break with traditional agricultural methods of growing mushrooms (point n in Figure 7-7, although in this case it is more of a societal constraint than incident). The company produces 1,000 tons of fresh mushrooms per year using high-tech techniques.[4] The high-tech methods include bioengineered ways of selecting the seeds for breeding, "intelligent" control of an artificially stimulative environment, and roboticized mechanical work. The mushrooms are grown in an "organic" way in the sense that pesticide, chemical fertilizers, and growth hormones are not used. The resulting mushrooms are kept fresh in a vacuum. Using these high-tech approaches, the company keeps growing mushrooms around the year with no off-season. The mushrooms are substantially exported to North America, Europe, Australia, and throughout southeast Asia, even though there is unsatisfied demand in the domestic Chinese market.

7.3 Three eras of change and management

While this book is almost totally about breakthrough management, we must look back briefly and provide some context for breakthrough management in terms of the two prior important paradigms for management: process control and incremental improvement.

The methods of process control were developed in the 1930s and 1940s in the U.S. and adopted with revolutionary effect by Japan in the 1950s. Process control is symbolically indicated in the left portion of Figure 7-10 by a flat line indicative of the goal of synchronizing and minimizing the variation of all of the parts of an industrial process so that mass production was possible. The methods of process control are now used by sophisticated businesses (and other institutions) throughout the world.

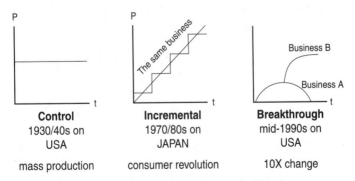

Figure 7-10. *Left: process control; middle: incremental improvement; right: breakthrough*

The revolutionary methods of incremental improvement were developed in Japan in the 1960s and 1970s. Incremental improvement is symbolically indicated by the staircase graph in the middle portion of Figure 7-10, indicative of the goal of incrementally and repeatedly improving the business' product or service offers and the processes for providing. As with process control, the methods of incremental improvement (for instance, the methods of lean production or Six Sigma) are now used by more-sophisticated businesses throughout the world.

The goals of process control and incremental improvement in their times were the same as the goal of breakthrough management today—to successfully compete and survive. Survival requires making money—at least sufficient money to cover costs and typically enough money to provide investors with a return on their investment.[5]

However, while process control was sufficient in the 1930s and 1940s for long-term survival, in the 1970s and 1980s a business could not count on long-term survival by only focusing on incremental improvement; incremental improvement was becoming an increasingly necessary condition but it was not a sufficient condition. Businesses still needed to maintain their skill at process control or their products and costs would not be sufficiently reliable to stay in business. Examples abound of companies going out of business because of inadequate process control. For instance, Shoji Shiba remembers that between the afternoon of March 1, 1955, and the morning of March 2, a total of 1936 students at nine elementary schools in Tokyo had serious stomach problems, including vomiting, from drinking Snow Brand milk products. The company had lost control of its manufacturing process on account of an electrical blackout and insufficient maintenance work and, thus, products from one of its plants caused food poisoning in the children. As a result, the chief executive had to resign. In another example, David Walden still is sad about the fate of his onetime favorite sourdough French bread, made in the 1960s by the Larabaru company in San Francisco; the company shipped some bread that poisoned and (Walden thinks he remembers) killed some customers and, thus, went out of business. The world-renowned Arthur Andersen accounting firm was forced out of business when it became clear that its internal controls on giving proper accounting advice were inadequate, if not explicitly ignored. You will be able to think up your own additional examples—perhaps close calls within your own business.

The same thing is true in today's era where companies are sometimes forced to seek new businesses (shown symbolically in the right portion of Figure 7-10). A company can switch businesses, but then the company has to deliver its products or services in a reliable, controlled way to get and keep customers; and sooner rather than later, it will probably have to provide incremental improvements to its products and services to remain competitive with other companies that are trying to expand in the same business area.

The connection between making money and survival is illustrated at the right side of Figure 7-11. The left side of the figure illustrates the necessity of having elements of process control (and its emphasis on standardization), incremental improvement (with its emphasis on continuing customer satisfaction based on ever-improvement levels of customer-perceived quality), and breakthrough management (with its emphasis on new market values through innovation).

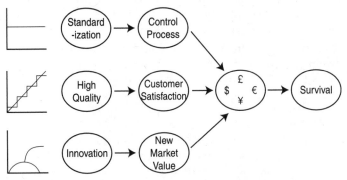

Figure 7-11. *Business logic of the three management paradigms*

The key trick is the relative timing of increased emphasis on each of the three elements shown in the figure. The importance of the three types of management has changed over the years as the *clock speed* of various industries has changed.[6] Clock speed is how fast things change in an industry. Charles Fine's book on the subject discusses three types of clock speed (product technology clock speed, organization clock speed, and process technology clock speed) and gives examples from various industries.

Twenty or thirty years ago, many leading industries had clock speeds mostly measured in tens or perhaps a hundred years or more, including aircraft, tobacco, steel, shipbuilding, petrochemical, paper, electricity, and diamond mining industries. Leading industries with product clock speeds mostly ranging from four to eight years and organization and process clock speeds ranging from five to twenty-five years included the bicycle, automobile, computer operating system, agriculture, fast food, beer brewing, and airline industries.

Today, the leading industries have product clock speeds mostly under a year (and no more than one to three years) and organization and process clock speeds of a few years to, at most, ten to twenty years.

Thus, many years ago it was sufficient to introduce a technology and then do control management for many years. A little more recently, say twenty years ago, one could introduce a new technology, do control management, and then add management of incremental improvement to remain competitive, as shown in the top part of Figure 7-12. One could alternate back and forth between incremental improvement and control for years until eventually a new breakthrough was needed to stay in business.

Today, management often must be done in a new way. One starts with a breakthrough, as shown in the bottom part of Figure 7-12, producing the new product as exactly as possible and getting it under control. From there one improves the product using the methods of incremental improvement, getting each change under control; but, surprisingly soon, one has to jump to the next breakthrough. In other words, faster clock speed in an industry means that breakthrough is required more often.

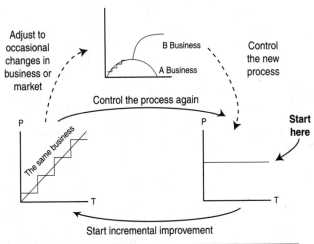

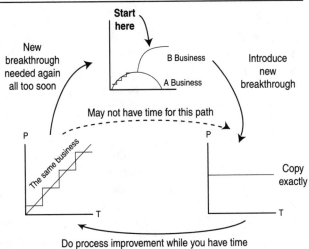

Figure 7-12. *Change in the frequency of use of breakthrough management*

Before we move on, we summarize and compare the characteristics of the three types of management using the chart in Figure 7-13.

	Control	**Incremental**	**Breakthrough**
	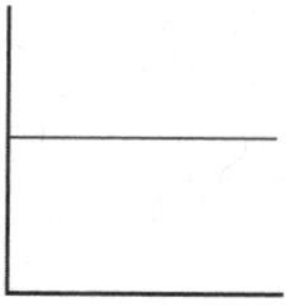	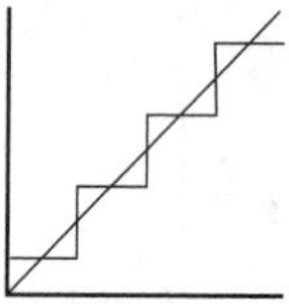	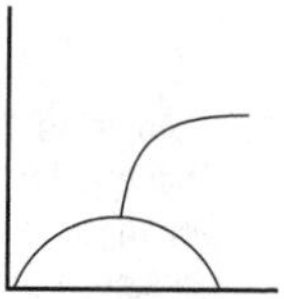
Change	Process	Standard	Business
Unchange	Standard	Business	Values
Hypothesis for Human Nature	Theory **X**	Theory **Y**	Theory **Z**
Key Player	Middle Manager	Shop Floor Workers	Top-Upper Managers
Management Focus	Discipline Focus	Backward Focus	Forward Focus
Data	Numeric	Numeric and Language	Language and Image
Tools	Statistical Analysis	Kaizen Methods	Explicit Image and Language Processing Methods

Figure 7-13. Comparison of the three paradigms of management

The second row of the table lists the "logic" of the various approaches to management that we already saw in Figure 7-11. In all three cases, making money is required for survival. In the control management paradigm, to make money one must control processes and to do that one must have standardization. In the paradigm for managing incremental improvement, making money requires customer satisfaction, which in turn requires a culture and systems for quality. The paradigm for management of breakthrough requires some new value to the market to make money, which in turn requires innovation in some dimension of the business.

The third row of Figure 7-13 shows what is unchanging and changing in the different methods of management. In control management, the standards may be unchanging while the process for achieving the standards changes to improve. In incremental improvement management, the business is more or less unchanging while the standards (i.e., characteristics of the product or service) change.

In breakthrough management, the company "values" are unchanging even though the type of business changes. This pattern can be seen with the various businesses we described earlier in this chapter. In each case the underlying company value was unchanged. The toothpaste company always did something related to the mouth as it repeatedly augmented the form of its business. Okamoto Glass always dealt with glass even though it dramatically changed its glass-making technology and areas of application. ASKUL always continued to address daily distribution of a commodity product as it went through its various business evolutions. The FAVI company we will describe in section 9.1 always stays focused on die casting even as it finds different areas of business (see Figure 9-1).

One can imagine how too big a jump to a new business could be so different that creativity to solve problems and create new ideas is decreased. For instance, one Japanese steel company had started a fish cultivation business to utilize hot water that was a by-product of the steel manufacturing process; but fish cultivation was too far from the original steel business, and the project failed. When faced with 10X change, a company foreseeing that it has to make an A-to-B jump would do well to think about the question, "What is our core, unchanging value?"

The next row of the figure lists theories of human nature and management. Theories X and Y are described in McGregor's book.[7] Theory X says that people want stability and to be led. It suggests the power of standardization and control of workers in the pursuit of mass production. Theory Y says people seek self-determination and innovation. It suggests the accrual of knowledge, continuous improvement, and worker development and empowerment in pursuit of creating something new. Theory Z is what Shoji Shiba calls his idea that in the quest for breakthrough we must move beyond rational thinking in some circumstances.

The fifth row of the figure shows who is important in the three types of management. Historically, leaders of organizations delegated control management to middle managers, and this was appropriate. Continuous improvement activities must be substantially focused among the workers themselves—that is where the information is for improvement, not at the top levels of the organization. However, management of breakthrough necessitates great attention of the leaders of organizations; no one but the leader can change the business. Thus, breakthrough management is a key skill for top managers and requires the top manager to build an appropriate system to accomplish breakthrough, a different paradigm than for either control management or incremental improvement management. The leader is also the most logical person to have the forward view called for in the next row of the figure.

The seventh row of the table indicates the types of data that are most relevant to the different types of management, and the eighth row indicates the types of tools most relevant for scientific analysis of the various types of data. While breakthrough management is a relatively new skill, it is not without tools, and in the next three chapters we describe eight useful principles.

We conclude this section by connecting the three types of management to a memorable visual image. In paintings relating to Buddhism, three eyes are sometimes shown. These are the eye of the past, eye of the present, and eye of wisdom. The three types of management, which today's CEOs must simultaneously be concerned with, can be illustrated as the three eyes in Buddhism, as shown in Figure 7-14.

The CEO needs an eye to monitor management for control, or else the company will not meet the minimum contract between the company and society. The CEO needs an eye to monitor management for incremental improvement, or else the company will not keep up with changing customer requirements today. The CEO needs the wisdom to see the part to future breakthrough, or else the company will have no tomorrow.

Figure 7-14. *Eyes of the past (right), present (left), and future (top middle)*

Notes

1. Andrew Grove, *Only the Paranoid Survive*, Currency Doubleday, paperback edition, 1999.

2. Katu-Koujou (The factory winning in competition), Yasuhiro Goto, Nihon Keizai shinbunsya, 2005.

3. This was also reported in Shiba01.

4. The detailed information in the rest of this paragraph comes from a brochure from the mushroom company that Shoji Shiba obtained when he visited the company in May 2005.

5. Peter Drucker famously noted that the goal of business is not making a profit; rather the goal of business is finding or creating and keeping customers by providing products or services they need. Profit, Drucker continued, is a cost of doing business, so the business can get the investors it needs.

6. Charles H. Fine. *Clock Speed: Winning Industry Control in the Age of Temporary Advantage*. Perseus Books, Reading, MA, 1998.

7. Douglas McGregor. *The Human Side of Enterprise*. McGraw-Hill, New York, 25th anniversary printing edition, 1985.

Chapter Eight

Identify Need

Many businesses have leaders, but only some of them are naturally, or circumstances compel them to be, concerned with transformation. Transformation requires vision that is not required of or does not come naturally to many more-traditional leaders and, thus, we call leaders of transformation "visionary leaders."

The visionary leader must work, more or less successively, in three major areas of effort, as shown in Figure 8-1.

This chapter and the next two chapters discuss the work of the visionary leader though the use of several case studies from real companies and institutions. Out of these case studies and others we have observed, we see eight principles of visionary leadership that the leaders in the cases we have studied generally hold in common. The eight principles are listed in Table 8-1.

The first two principles are introduced in this chapter on identifying the need. Principles 3–5 are introduced in Chapter 9 on initiating the transformation. Principles 6–8 are introduced in Chapter 10 on building the new business.

While each case study focuses on a subset of the eight principles, Tables 10-1 through 10-6 at the end of Chapter 10 summarize the application of all eight principles in each case study. Naturally, there is overlap among the applications of the principles in the various case studies and some cases do not provide clear, strong examples of some of the principles.

The rest of this chapter addresses the first task shown in Figure 8-1—identification of the transformational needs. There are two aspects of this: 1) identifying the need for transformation, and 2) identifying what transformation is needed. This is a process of discovering what is unknown or invisible and turning it into a commitment for tangible change in a visible direction.

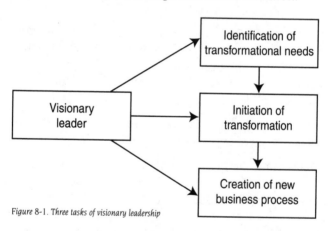

Figure 8-1. *Three tasks of visionary leadership*

Table 8-1. Eight principles of visionary leadership

Principle 1. The visionary leader must do on-site observation leading to *personal perception* of changes in *societal values* from an *outsider's point of view*.

Principle 2. Even though there is resistance, *never give up*; squeeze the resistance between *outside-in* pressure in combination with top-down inside instruction.

Principle 3. Transformation is begun with *symbolic disruption* of old or traditional systems through *top-down* efforts to *create chaos* within the organization.

Principle 4. The direction of transformation is illustrated aimed by a symbolic *visible image* and the visionary leader's *symbolic behavior*.

Principle 5. Quickly establishing new *physical, organizational*, and *behavioral systems* is essential for successful transformation.

Principle 6. *Real change leaders* are necessary to enable transformation.

Principle 7. Create an *innovative* system to provide *feedback from results*.

Principle 8. Create a daily operation system including the new *work structure*, new approach to *human capabilities*, and *improvement activities*.

8.1 Humanitas and Principle 1

Principle 1. The visionary leader must do on-site observation leading to *personal perception* of changes in *societal values* from an *outsider's point of view*.

Three components of this principle are highlighted in italics. The visionary leader needs to see things from the point of view of an outsider. The visionary leader needs to do on-site (by which we mean firsthand) observation that leads to a personal perception. As an outsider, looking at things firsthand, the visionary leader has the best chance to sense a change in societal value that can lead to new opportunities. Hans Becker and his work at Humanitas provide a good example of this principle.

In October 21, 2005, Shoji Shiba and Mr. Bertrand Jouslin de Noray, Secretary General of the European Organization for Quality (www.eoq.org), visited Humanitas in the Rotterdam district of the Netherlands and met with CEO Hans Becker, among other people.[1]

The Humanitas Foundation is a nonprofit organization that provides housing and home care for elderly people. More than 6,000 elderly people live in Humanitas apartments, and the company employs about 2,100 people. It also utilizes 900 volunteers. It is one of the largest institutions in this field in the Netherlands.

Historical perspective on eldercare

In historical times, elderly people typically remained living with their extended families, often still in their lifelong homes, and members of their extended families took care of the elders when they no longer could take care of themselves (and the elders were at least theoretically respected and looked on as a source of wisdom). There was also not so much that was complicated that medical science could do for aging and sick people, and general practitioner doctors made house calls; so, staying at home through a person's final decline in health to death made sense.

In more recent times, people have lived to older ages, medical practice has gotten more complicated and doctors stopped making house calls, and families often have become geographically distributed. This has resulted in the development of special facilities to take care of the elderly people who needed rehabilitation after hospitalization or who could no longer live by themselves at home. These "nursing homes" looked like and ran like something closer to hospitals than homes, often with two, four, or six residents to a room with only thin curtains providing visual (and no audio) privacy. Few people want to live in nursing homes. Most people's ideal is to continue living at home as they grow old and ill.

More recently (at least in the U.S.), a type of facility called an assisted living facility developed that was aimed at providing a more homey feeling—buildings with small apartments partially furnished with the residents' own household items (beds, dressers, chairs, TVs, etc.) and with assistance from the facility staff for routine tasks such as clothes washing, food preparation, room cleaning, and reminders to take medicines. Sometimes these assisted living facilities are located on the same campus with a) independent-living apartments for recent retirees (typically in a separate building or at least in a separate wing), and b) skilled nursing facilities (almost certainly in a separate building) for those who are too disabled to remain in assisted living; and the institution's marketing brochures describe a smooth transition from independent living to assisted living to skilled nursing.

However, such assisted living facilities have their own problems. Too often they, too, feel quite institutional rather than like home. They run like institutions with meals at certain times, all residents in equally poor health, artificial recreational activities such as bingo and group crafts, and a lot of rules and standards. In particular (again, at least in the U.S.), they are subject to many government healthcare regulations as well as business positioning and staff certification constraints such that an assisted living resident often is evicted at some point and forced into a nursing home because of an ailment or lack of capability that should not inherently prevent them from being cared for in their assisted living facility.

Thus, in effect, elderly people who decide (or their families decide for them) that they should give up their homes and move to a retirement community, tend to lose control of their lives sooner than they expect. As they grow infirm, they are told they must leave the multiroom independent living apartments that were an attractive alternative to their own homes and move to a separate assisted living facility. In so doing, they again incur much of the emotional pain of giving up friendly neighbors and another significant portion of their belongings. They typically move to a one-room (or studio) apartment, and often are second-class citizens when it comes to food service (that may be an adjunct to the food service for the independent living residents). Then, having hopefully adjusted to their new home and fellow residents in assisted living, they may be told that they no longer qualify for assisted living, and have 30 days to leave and find a skilled nursing facility somewhere. Once in a skilled nursing facility, in the U.S., Medicare will only pay for two-person rooms (not a private room), labor economics inevitably prevent staffing at a sufficient level to allow sufficient individualized care for all patients, and healthcare regulations (e.g., railings on beds must be up to prevent a person from falling out of bed) can almost imprison the patient. Thus, after three home changes (in perhaps as many years), the elderly person ends up in a completely un-home-like setting where he or she may reside until death in a number of years. There will be no provision for a person's spouse to live with them in a nursing home. It's no wonder that as one walks down the halls of a typical skilled nursing facility, you not-infrequently hear a patient plaintively and endlessly calling "help, help..." Curiously, the less home-like and more oppressive the facility becomes, the more expensive it also becomes.

Evolution of Humanitas

In the years before 1990, the facilities of Humanitas were like those of many other eldercare facilities in the Netherlands. The healthcare professionals ran the show and focused narrowly on the physical health of the patients rather than on their overall well-being and happiness. Six to eight people lived together in large rooms. There was a "do this, do that" culture with a lot of standard procedures. Everyone ate meals at the same times, everyone had the same kind of cleaning, etc.

Today, Humanitas has implemented a revolutionary approach for the living arrangements for elderly people. The new concept is based on four ideas:[2]

▶ Age-proof residential complexes

▶ Supporting self-determination and self-reliance among clients (as Humanitas calls them, instead of calling them patients)

▶ Extended family concept

▶ Supporting fun through positive attitude, surroundings, and atmosphere

These ideas are aimed at moving Humanitas from a culture focusing fairly exclusively on health care (in an institutional setting) to a culture that has a less-institutional feel and "focuses" on care, attractive housing, and the overall well-being of the residents.

Age-proof residential complexes. By 2004, Humanitas has demolished five old residence buildings and built 10 new residential complexes. The new facilities look more like modern hotels than old age residences. (See the three photos of Figure 8-2 showing building views.) The apartments in each residential complex are pleasant and adequately roomy—a minimum of 70 square meters (which is a little over 750 square feet), or larger for more wealthy people. A resident can rent or buy. A person or couple over 55 years of age can move to a Humanitas facility while they are still in relatively good health and make it their "residence for life." Humanitas manages the residency of each complex to maintain a desired balance between residents who require no care, those who need some care, and those who need full care.

These complexes are like little villages (as with many modern hotels) containing restaurants, supermarkets, hairdressers and beauty salons and other types of shops, Internet cafes with computer classes, bars where a person can buy drinks, baby and child care facilities open to outsiders, laundries, gyms, and so on.

Apartments are designed to accommodate residents if they grow less able (e.g., including "handicapped" accessibility, "help" call buttons, central monitoring in case a resident forgets to turn things off after cooking, etc.). The able residents and the less-able residents can be and are mixed throughout a complex.

With such attractive and "residence for life" facilities, there is strong demand for people to move to them (in 2004 there was a 12,000-person and at least six-month waiting list) and to make the apartments their permanent homes earlier rather than later (i.e., rather than holding out until the last possible moment in the person's house and then having to go to a skilled nursing facility). As a resident grows older and perhaps less able, the resident stays in the same apartment, and additionally needed health care and housework is provided on an a la carte basis without requiring the resident to move. There are (slightly hidden) physical, occupational and speech therapy, dentist, doctor, and nursing home facilities within the complex. Even residents that come to suffer from dementia are more likely to be able to stay in their "residence for life" apartments if the apartments have become their accustomed homes before they begin to suffer from dementia. As hospitals in the Netherlands become increasing specialized to providing intensive treatment, Humanitas is already beginning to provide real hospital functions for residents with diabetes, asthma, fractures, hernias, cerebral hemorrhages, need for kidney dialysis, eye or ear disorders, heart conditions, and stomach and intestinal complaints.[3]

In summary, the Humanitas approach to avoiding making older people move from home to unpleasant living facilities is to provide pleasant living facilities that can become home and stay a person's home for the rest of the person's life.

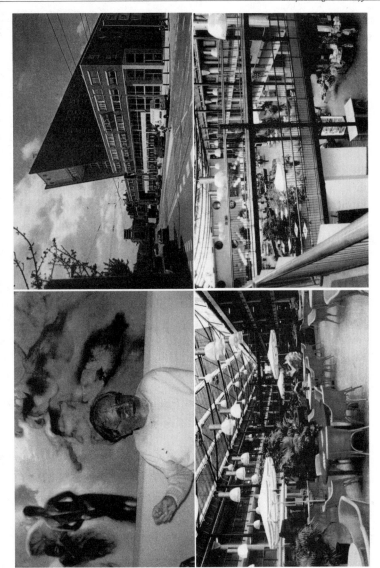

Figure 8-2. *Hans Becker and views of a Humanitas building*

Supporting self-determination and self-reliance among clients. Traditional assisted living and nursing homes (certainly in the U.S.) have some rules policies (probably for liability protection or government health regulation reasons) that encourage residents to become more dependent. In contrast, Humanitas has the slogan, "use it or lose it" (which we suppose applies to both physical independence and a feeling of independence). Humanitas' policy is to encourage maximum possible self-reliance and self-determination of the residents. Residents taking more care of themselves (or each other in the case of couples, or with the aid of family members), up to the "pain threshold," helps them maintain a sense of independence (physical and otherwise) and in practice postpones increasing levels of dependence. This brings greater happiness to the residents and significant economic benefits to Humanitas; Humanitas doesn't have to do what a resident or the resident's spouse can do. Humanitas also encourages its residents to help each other. All this may seem a bit exploitive upon first examination (a 100-year-old woman at one Humanitas complex cooks and makes her bed every day), until we think about older people in the world at large and how they struggle to stay independent and living in their homes and perhaps help other elderly neighbors when they can barely do things for themselves. Younger people often talk about what "is best" for elderly people (i.e., safe from injury and not a worry to the young people), but often the older people don't want this for themselves.

Extended family concept. Elderly, sick people are not allowed to be isolated in Humanitas facilities. All sorts of people live together in a "neighborhood." The apartments of "sick and healthy people, old and young, poor and rich, immigrant and Dutch" are all mixed together.

The Humanitas complex healthcare facilities are open to residents from the outside neighborhood as are the shops and community gathering spaces of a Humanitas complex. In particular, each Humanitas complex includes a good restaurant to attract people from the surrounding city to meet and talk. Shoji Shiba visited one restaurant for lunch, and it was a wonderful high-class restaurant. Humanitas advertises and promotes these restaurants.

Having such facilities available to the outside world provides some economic benefit to Humanitas. More importantly, it provides greater richness to the internal and external community, including musical performances, bridge tournaments, and food festivals, and makes them stakeholders in each other. In other words, the Humanitas residents are an integral part of a large community just as a person is who lives in his or her own home. Residents, families, staff, volunteers, and neighbors in the surrounding neighborhood all increasingly see it as just another part of town life. We can imagine that having normal city retail establishments within the Humanitas complex also leads to more visits from family and friends of residents. Visiting someone in an isolated assisted living or skilled nursing facility might require a special trip that might happen infrequently; visiting someone in a Humanitas complex might be piggybacked onto normal daily shopping, getting a haircut, etc., and thus might happen more frequently.

Humanitas also encourages volunteer efforts among the residents of their complexes.

The extended family idea (along with age-proof apartments and self-reliance) works to avoid a patient-undergoing-medical-treatment mentality of care at Humanitas. Old style nursing and assisted living facilities tend to create patient/medical-treatment relationships. Humanitas transforms the traditional concept to one where the extended family of nurses, nurses aides, personal care assistants, actual family members, and volunteers all belong to the family of the resident. Volunteer helpers are a kind of new family member. Humanitas is trying to create a new type of social link.

Supporting fun through positive attitude, surroundings, and atmosphere. Much of what was discussed under the preceding three points also relates to this point. We will get into this point more deeply (but still somewhat implicitly) in the next subsection about Hans Becker.

Hans Becker

Hans Becker, Ph.D., is the visionary leader of Humanitas. (See his photo in Figure 8-2.) When he was recruited to become the general manager of Humanitas in about 1992, his impression of residences for the elderly was that they were "misery islands" (as Dr. Becker's elderly father called them) or "bureaucratic horrors" (as described by the controversial Dutch politician Pim Fortuyn). Humanitas was no exception to the "misery island" characterization. However:

> ...Humanitas had formulated their goals as follows: "The foundation provides services to those in need, to whom the freedom to act in accordance with their own beliefs and convictions is guaranteed, and based on the integrity of the human being, who is being held responsible to himself and to his fellow human beings." This official Humanitas statement formulated in 1969 (!) offered many opportunities for improvement. So Becker joined Humanitas and started the transformation process.[4]

The beginning of Hans Becker's journey at Humanitas closely matches our Principle 1. Becker had an outsider's view of Humanitas—he was headhunted into joining Humanitas. He knew what faced most people who were not wealthy as they grew old; he had observed the current eldercare system "on-site" via his own middle-class background and his elderly father's perspective. He must have sensed (or perhaps thought about it explicitly as a university graduate in the history of economics) that the time might have been ripe for a demonstration of change in societal values regarding eldercare; otherwise we doubt he would have taken the Humanitas job.

One of the facility directors Shoji Shiba talked to said that she had been with the organization for 25 years, and nothing changed before Dr. Becker arrived. Becker's attitude and approach was very different. He stated that elderly people were not ill. Rather, they needed help; in particular, they needed happiness. Nutritious food and good cleanliness was not enough for happiness. Atmosphere including noise, smell, and mess/chaos was necessary. A rum chop might be much more helpful than medical care. Becker asserted that Humanitas' job was to protect senior people from the "medical mafia"—those who primarily think of care in terms of good application of the medical code. Becker instituted a no-white-jackets culture. Also, humans need to be bosses of their own lives and control their own life. But, traditional eldercare practice says, "We can provide dinner only at 5p.m., and we can provide only the same coffee."[5] Becker asserted that in facilities with four people to a room, run like they are primarily enforcing a medical code, family members will not visit long and will mostly remember the smell of urine. Becker believes it is important to talk about things other than being old and ill. At Humanitas there are many paintings around the walls of the building (see bottom right of Figure 8-2). In Becker's view these need not be beautiful as long as they trigger interesting conversation.

Dr. Becker made many other changes. He immediately stopped the work of outside consultants such as McKinsey & Company. (Apparently, the consultants were providing marketing and strategic direction help.) He moved to pull down an old building and began building innovative buildings such as we have described. He got rid of most meetings, which he thinks are a waste of time in 90 percent of the cases and tend to be overly theoretical, preferring enthusiastic individual initiative and actual experiments that often will give immediate good results. According to Becker, a meeting is needed in only 10 percent of the cases.

Dr. Becker initiated what Humanitas calls the "yes culture." The Humanitas staff members' response to ideas, suggestions, or requests from residents or other stakeholders in the institution is supposed to assume the answer is "yes" rather than to check why it might not be possible. Of course, in some few instances, the answer will have to be "no," but assume "yes." Becker says that 90 percent of the time the answer can be "yes," but it is easier for people to start by assuming and saying "no." For instance, suppose a resident said he or she wanted to have five cats in an apartment, or suppose a resident said he wanted to have a prostitute (not illegal in the Netherlands) come to his apartment; it's something that a person could have in his or her own home, so why not in an apartment for life in Humanitas. (In general, Humanitas seems accepting of reasonable pets, and Becker's five-year plan includes encouraging more animals.)

Dr. Becker believes the yes culture enhances creativity, although it sometimes creates chaos. On the other hand, even chaos sometimes leads to benefits. For example, some residents wanted to have a circus come into a Humanitas building, and the answer was "yes." But an elephant came with the circus and the building staff was worried about the weight of the elephant and the floor—there was a little chaos. However, as a result all of the residents talked and talked about this event for a long time. A potentially negative situation was converted to positive talk and memories.

Most of the Humanitas staff were initially against these changes. Twenty or thirty percent of the medical staff left the organization. There were also big risks in the first several years. Becker pulled down an existing building in contravention to some Rotterdam city planning policies. The restaurant lost money in the first year. There was conflict with the social security system of Holland (and, even now, years later, Becker says Humanitas puts 10 percent of its efforts into control required by governmental regulations). It was three years before Becker could begin to justify his actions with good results.

In the face of the early opposition and in his leadership of Humanitas' continuing transformation, Dr. Becker's job is to continually emphasize the desired direction of change. Becker does this through talk and action. He and others on the management team keep the Humanitas story down to earth and vibrant and tell it often: he talks of "feeding five cats," "a rumchop is much better than medical treatment," "it is good to enjoy wine if you want," and "a beer a day keeps the doctor away." Becker also gets personally involved with resident issues; during Shoji Shiba's visit, Becker repeatedly interrupted things to deal with a resident's personal problem.

In addition to telling and acting out the Humanitas story within the organization, Dr. Becker also uses outside-in communication. For instance, seven years ago, Becker broke his leg and was hospitalized in a Humanitas apartment. A journalist visited him while he was in bed. Becker told the journalist of his complaints as a client of Humanitas: all he could see from his bed was the ceiling, the ceiling was dirty, his choice of food was very limited and he wasn't allowed to decide on his own preference for food, and the wine was not cold enough. These complaints were reported publicly. While in bed Becker talked to 200 different people. Becker is popular in the healthcare world in the Netherlands and, thus, he often appears on TV on a Humanitas-owned channel and other channels.

The Humanitas yes culture and its embracing of individual initiatives includes no daily systematic feedback system. Rather it depends on dealing with "moments of truth" (opportunities to satisfy or dissatisfy a customer, as coined by Jan Carlzon, onetime CEO of the Scandinavian Airlines System). At any time, residents can give suggestions and complaints to building directors and to Becker. Becker says that old people often complain, but it is important to find the causes behind the complaints: the complaint about bland food may well be accurate. Once a year, the director of a building complex meets formally with a group of residents.

Dr. Becker showed his five-year plan for Humanitas to Shoji Shiba. In Shiba's analysis, the plan addresses five general areas:

▶ Daily operations—increase the number of animals, add a fitness club for elderly people, make the restaurants more competitive, add attractive new features to the complexes such as a swimming pool and museum

▶ Challenges of new social problems—Alzheimer's clients, care for young handicapped people, hospice care for young people

▶ Investigation of the future value of the organization—integration of norms and values, evolving issues relating to human life

▶ Web technology—e-health, telemedicine

▶ Employee issues—the social security system of employees

Becker always looks outside Humanitas for information relating to the future vision of Humanitas.

8.2 ZIN and Principle 2

Principle 2. Even though there is resistance, *never give up*; squeeze the resistance between *outside-in* pressure in combination with top-down inside instruction.

Whenever someone tries to do something new in a company, there is always resistance. Employees don't like change, suppliers don't like change, customers don't like change, and observers are doubtful about change. In general, people don't like, don't believe, or can't see the benefit of change. How often has a new idea been called the proponent's "folly"? Thus, a leader who sees the need to transform his or her business or institution must have enormous determination and must never succumb to the temptation to give up; otherwise the leader will surely fail.

We saw the never-give-up principle in the Humanitas case study of the previous section. Dr. Becker was headhunted in particular for his strong commitment, based partly on his father's viewpoint about "misery islands." In the first year the restaurant lost money, and there was strong resistance from the staff, particularly the doctors, but Becker persevered, including such drastic actions as knocking down a building.

In the case study of Maeda in section 10.1, we will also see an excellent example of the never-give-up principle. Dr. Maeda, the CEO of the Maeda Corporation, had an idea for a new type of cement mixer based on folding dough in Dr. Maeda's hobby of making Japanese noodles. Such an idea seems silly on the face of it; additionally, Dr. Maeda is not an engineer by training, and his expert engineers were completely dismissive of Dr. Maeda's ideas. Nonetheless, as you will read in the case study, Dr. Maeda persevered.

Historic mission of mercy

Now let's look at the case study of ZIN, an institution that Shoji Shiba visited with Bertrand Jouslin de Noray, Secretary General of the EOQ, on October 20, 2005. ZIN has a significantly spiritual mission—to provide mercy. ZIN's visionary leader, Wim Verschuren, needed determination, repeated efforts at redirection and rebuilding, and a never-give-up attitude on a for-the-ages scale.[6]

The story of ZIN starts in the sixteenth century when an anonymous artist known as the Master of Alkmaar painted seven panels for the main church of Alkmaar, depicting seven works of mercy. (Today this artwork is in the Rijksmuseum in Amsterdam.) This church ornamentation was related to a larger movement of mercy that happened in the sixteenth century in reaction to poverty and war and in keeping with Matthew 25 in the Bible:[7]

> [verse 34] Then the King will say to those at his right hand, "Come, O blessed of my Father, inherit the kingdom prepared for you from the foundation of the world;
>
> [verse 35] for I was hungry and you gave me food, I was thirsty and you gave me drink, I was a stranger and you welcomed me,

[verse 36] I was naked and you clothed me, I was sick and you visited me, I was in prison and you came to me."

In the early nineteenth century there was a revival of the ideal of mercy in reaction to the industrial revolution making paupers of many people and people who were paupers because of discrimination. Bishop Joannes Zwijsen, who had founded the Sisters of Charity in 1832, founded in Tilburg the Brothers of Mary, Mother of Mercy (also known as the Brothers CMM) in 1845. This Roman Catholic order of brothers had the mission to serve the poor. (See http://www.cmmbrothers.nl/english/index.htm for some details of the history and current activities of the Brothers CMM.) In the following 90 years, the order spread around the Netherlands province of Noord-Brabant and to Belgium (1851), Surinam (1902), Indonesia (1923), Kenya (1958), Namibia (1958), California (1963), and Brazil (1980). The brothers' vocations often involved education of young (and sometimes secondary school) children, particularly children with handicaps such as deafness and blindness.

However, by the middle of the 1900s, "mercy" was a word no longer much heard in the Netherlands, and when it was heard it had a negative undertone. Also, as times changed, fewer men joined the order, the existing members of the order grew older and retired from day-to-day teaching, and by the end of the 1970s the order had substantially lost its inspiration and identity, at least in the Netherlands. (Today the future of the Brothers CMM as a traditional religious order lies mostly in Indonesia, Africa, and perhaps Brazil.)

Wim Verschuren

Wim Verschuren was born in 1933. His father was a farmer who was killed in WWII when Wim was nine years old. At age 18, Wim joined the Brothers CMM. Brother Wim says that at that time the Brothers CMM had a culture of "bow and obedience"; for example, a brother might get a letter from the order headquarters saying that the brother had been replaced in his current assignment and was to move within three days to his next assignment. In the Brothers CMM, Brother Wim became an elementary school teacher, and at age 24 he was teaching kids at an institute for the blind, working day and night, seven days a week.

Then, suddenly, Brother Wim's life changed. He was ordered to go to university, which was unusual since previously brothers had not been permitted to go to university. At university, he studied pedagogy, and then he taught in a teacher training college. Brother Wim could have remained teaching at the college level, but he was appointed a member of the board of the Brothers CMM order, and so he left academia and served the order directly again, from 1968 on. This was a time when a number of brothers and sisters in many religious orders were giving up their vocations and returning to lay life. Many of Brother Wim's own colleagues were leaving the order. When he was appointed to the board, he intuitively said, "yes," and decided to remain in the order, and the renewed commitment gave him energy and freedom to do new things.

In the later 1970s, Brother Wim was appointed to be superior general of the Brothers CMM. As superior general of the order, Brother Wim spent a lot of time in Africa and Indonesia, helping diffuse the vocation of mercy. Part of the revitalization of the order in Africa and Indonesia was to pull down some existing schools and to start new schools from scratch, which was something of a shock for the entire order. In 1990 Wim retired from his service as superior general. In his view, he had done a lot in Africa and Indonesia and now it was time to do more in Europe. In particular, there was a growing crisis in the order in the Netherlands.

Brother Wim wrote:

> We had lost our identity and our inspiration due to the fundamental changes in church and society. The result being, that

we threatened also to lose each other and that our sound self-respect began to fade. I experienced this crisis personally as an executive, as a member of the board of our congregation. Being aware of the fact that my community and I were only able to overcome this crisis by renewing our spirituality, we started a process of re-sourcing. And in its course we rediscovered mercy as if it were a precious stone that we had to find first and subsequently remove a lot of dust before we could see how beautiful and colorful it was. It took many years before we recovered a new identity and pride in mercy and before it became a guideline in our everyday life and work and in leadership.

When we celebrated our 150th anniversary in 1994, we gave publicity to what we had experienced to be of vital importance. Being old, we wanted to pass this heritage on, in the conviction that mercy is more than ever relevant to our present society. Much to our surprise, it was well received by individuals and by groups. Moreover, it appears that people in some other places in the Netherlands were working on a revaluation of mercy.

Essentially, the order had understood that mercy was still a relevant concept, and they needed to embrace it again and find contemporary approaches to practicing it.

A renewed movement of mercy

With the order having reembraced its mission to provide mercy, in 1998 Brother Wim had the somewhat surprising idea to put a recruiting advertisement in the newspaper saying that the Brothers CMM were looking for men to join them as brothers, with no possibility of marriage, conventional careers, or money; the ad also asked for "allies [laypeople, nonbrothers] in the movement for mercy." This ad caught the public's attention via TV and newspaper reports, and people applied.

Understanding that they were on to something, Brother Wim led the Brothers CMM's effort to launch, starting in December 1998, an explicit movement of mercy. In the years that followed, the movement of mercy grew beyond expectations. Brother Wim Verschuren led these activities until he stepped down as chairman of the board of the movement of mercy at a semi-annual meeting at the ZIN facility in Vught on November 5, 2005.

ZIN center in Vught

The Brothers CMM have had to close a number of their locations over the years as brothers have aged and died and few new men have joined the brotherhood and apparently society needed less of the services the order provided. However, when it came to the church and residence for brothers in Vught (near the founding location of Tilburg), they did not want to sell the property to others. In particular, this was the location of a cemetery containing the graves of 900 brothers.

Brother Wim met with hundreds of people as he investigated possible ways for the order to hold onto this property. In particular, he was acquainted with a man named Leendert Bikker who was part of a consultation and marketing venture. This man connected Brother Wim with various people in industry, and eventually a sort of joint venture came about with Leendert Bikker that would allow the Vught property to be redeveloped and reused with the brothers still involved. The Brothers CMM were able to provide their share of the investment because they had funds that had come from the sale of an old elementary school.

They built a modern new building attached to the church that provided conference facilities, with the church being an integral part of the new complex. Once this construction was done, a new residential building was built for the brothers who still lived there, and the brother's old residential building was torn down. The conference center, although a commercial entity, was designed and organized to maintain strong ties with the Brothers CMM and their traditions of providing mercy.

The complex is now know as the "Zin in Werk" center (or ZIN for short), where the name has to do with finding meaning (zin) in work or in life more generally. A premise is that in modern life people are having increasing trouble balancing personal, family, and work needs. They may not like what they do for work, but they have to make money to support their families. Also, links within the family may have become weak, for a variety of reasons. Brother Wim believes that society needs to create a new system to balance work life, spiritual life, and family life. He also believes the key is not money but relations among people. (He feels the brothers have considerable insight about relations among people: they explicitly joined knowing they will live in communities, the younger brothers take care of the brothers who are growing old, and they also revere and take care of the grave sites of the brothers who have died.)

ZIN markets itself particularly to groups of people from the worlds of education, care services, and government—groups that are interested in helping address important current problems in the Netherlands. There are three types of customers of ZIN. Some customers merely rent the physical facilities and hold their own activities. Some customers hire a combination of an outside expert and members of the ZIN staff to give training, for example, police officer training, Catholic leadership training, spiritual facilitator training, facilitator training for people dealing with kids with mental problems, etc. Finally, sometimes a conference organizer rents the facility and ZIN provides instructors, for instance, for personality training.

The physical facilities are an integral part of the ZIN package. There are 38 rooms for staying overnight, a dining room, and conference rooms (Figure 8-3). All are simple, but clean and comfortable. The more-traditional monastic cloister environ-

Figure 8-3. Brother Wim and a typical ZIN overnight room, dining room, and conference room

ment is also available to the guests, who are encouraged to spend time in it and understand its symbolism (Figure 8-4).

Figure 8-4. ZIN environment emphasizes the spiritual: church with copies of the Master of Alkmaar's paintings of the Seven Works of Mercy, cemetery, garden, and meditation room

The economics of ZIN have not been easy. They had a loss in 2000, and in 2003 a foundation that was providing financial support stopped. However, they persevered. By late 2005 they were nearly full all the time; and ZIN's director, Henk-Jan Hoefman, is improving the business side of ZIN. He has two sections that work for him: 1) the context section that deals with overnight accommodations, food, conference rooms, cleaning, etc., and 2) the content section that works with clients on development of programs. He utilizes the "brothers' spirit" in the context section (two brothers work in ZIN), but uses outside professionals for the content part. Hoefman personally does not like marketing and says that everyone involved must be a marketing manager. He has a clear business model for ZIN: 1) focus on topics relating to spirituality and a combination of business and spirituality, 2) use the brother's spirit (for environmental context) and outside professionals (for content) to complement each other, and 3) find links between and integrate realistic daily life with economic life and spiritual reflection. From these facts we can see that Director Hoefman has a different view of how ZIN should function while adopting the concept of the visionary leader, Brother Wim.

Brother's Wim's methods

From the descriptions in the preceding subsections, you can see that Brother Wim never gives up (Principle 2), even in the face of the most profound and relentless societal changes in values. He just keeps working on "re-creation."

When asked about his approach to revitalizing activities, Brother Wim explained that he always works on "re-creation" and that may be his talent—to rebuild an organization that has deep problems. He noted that he rebuilt the order's activities in Kenya and Indonesia, revived the movement of mercy, and rebuilt the church at Vught. Regarding specific success factors, Brother Wim noted:

- Vision is important—I am not a person of analysis, but my colleague, the director, is a very analytical person

- Take a risk—we often want to control the future and, if we cannot control it, we avoid deciding; but a leader needs to decide something, with courage and vision

- Flexibility—sometimes things go differently than we originally intended, but you need to be flexible enough to change your road to the goal

- Facts speak—concrete results tell you the truth; you need to see both good ideas and results

- Belonging to a community and fulfilling your responsibilities—in the Brothers CCM, religion provides cohesiveness among people; without a foundation of cohesiveness, it is impossible to accomplish your goal

- Involve the right people—you need people with different skills who embrace your goal

Brother Wim also has a strong belief in a brand image, and the ZIN center works to maintain a high-level brand image. They maintain on display a painting loaned to them by an important insurance company and valued at a million guilders. They have a huge grounds (seven hectares, or almost 43 acres, or about one-sixth of a square kilometer) that are a pleasure to walk through or look at, as shown in Figure 8-4. They held a competition of three famous architects to construct the new building and integrate it with the church. The building looks good inside (bamboo floors and wooden walls) and outside and won an architecture prize.

Outside-in communication

While a leader may have the determination to never give up, there is also little point in knocking directly on doors that will not be opened to you. There is a tendency for messages following the traditional path from the top of the organization to the bottom of the organization (left side of the Figure 8-5) to be ignored—"just more attempted manipulation from the top," employees may think. No matter how much the leader explains and cajoles and no matter how carefully the leader acts to be consistent with his words, people in the organization who do not want to change will resist (and even be cynical about) his example. Surprisingly, an often more-effective way to get the attention of one's own organization is to arrange things so the desired information and pressure comes from the outside world back to the people in the organization. Toward this end, some leaders take their ideas to the world at large, where they may be reflected back to the organization (right side of the figure).

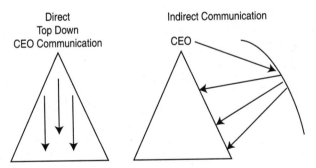

Figure 8-5. *Direct versus indirect communication*

In the case study of Humanitas in section 8.1, Dr. Becker used outside-in indirect communication methods including talking with journalists about his own experiences while he was hospitalized in a Humanitas apartment and through regular promotion of the Humanitas story on TV.

Andy Grove has written a book, *Only the Paranoid Survive* [Grove99], that describes his image of how the company has to deal with listening more to its customers. This book became famous and was widely read. Consequently, people inside the company undoubtedly were motivated to read the book and, thus, know much more about what Grove thought than they would ever have learned from internal memos and presentations. (Imagine what would have happened had he sent a book-length internal "memo" to all employees.)

Some years ago, Dr. Koji Kobayashi at NEC did the same thing when he was trying to promote the convergence of computers and communications. He wrote books that were published and widely read (and translated into English as well); thus, everyone in his own company also read them and knew what he thought needed to happen.[8]

We suspect that Bill Gates' books [Gates96, Gates99] served a similar purpose—communicating Gates' vision of an Internet-based future to the world at large but also to the employees within Microsoft, at a time when Microsoft was behind in its Internet orientation.

Each of three times Dr. Maeda visited MIT to present his case study (see section 10.1), he published a brochure telling the story of his visit and presentation of the story at MIT. This brochure was sent to customers and others in the world outside Dr. Maeda's company. However, by making this information available to customers, the information also undoubtedly spread through the company's own employees without necessarily seeming to be a lecture from the CEO.

Certainly Brother Wim's Netherlands-wide movement of mercy was an indirect way of addressing his own brothers and the potential users of the ZIN facilities about the need to embrace a modern interpretation of mercy and to make use of modern facilities and training to better apply the concepts of mercy to others and oneself.

Shoji Shiba saw a slightly different approach to indirect communication in China. The CEO of the ZTE company, a maker of telecommunications equipment, spent the equivalent of $15,000 per year (big money in China) to buy three books each month to distribute to all managers. The books related to the business and the philosophy of the CEO. Each manager was required to talk about the books four hours a week with their subordinates. Hopefully the subordinates began to remember the common language of change represented in the books the CEO carefully selected. We can imagine that the managers could hardly help but be the most influenced by this process.

8.3 Reflection

Principle 1. The visionary leader must do on-site observation leading to *personal perception* of changes in *societal values* from an *outsider's point of view*.

and

Principle 2. Even though there is resistance, *never give up*; squeeze the resistance between *outside-in* pressure in combination with top-down inside instruction.

Thinking again about the first task shown in Figure 8-1 and about Principles 1 and 2, the first job of the visionary manager can be illustrated as in Figure 8-6; to perceive the invisible societal change and then to identify what the transformational needs are. From both of these activities, the visionary leader needs to form a strong belief of the fact of the societal change and philosophy of how the business should be transformed; this belief and vision need to be so strong that the leader will not give up in the face of the inevitable resistance to change.

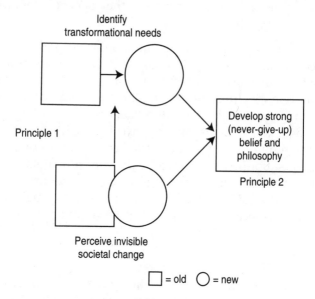

Figure 8-6. Essence of Principles 1 and 2

Notes

1. The information on Humanitas in this section comes from that visit, from a Humanitas brochure entitled "The Humanitas Foundation in a Nutshell (©2003/2005 by Stichting Humanitas), and from Marrewijk04.

2. Marrewijk04.

3. This sentence is only slightly paraphrased from the 2003/2005 brochure by Stichting Humanitas.

4. Marrewijk04.

5. Traditional eldercare in the U.S. also puts keeping a patient safe from injury above the happiness of the patient. For instance, a patient who takes a fall but is unhurt may be discouraged from continuing to walk and encouraged to use a wheelchair for fear that the person will fall again and break something. This is despite the fact that everyone, of any age, takes a spill from time to time and perhaps sometimes breaks something. But many elderly people would not give up the freedom to walk in order to be more safe from falls.

   At Humanitas they support further degrees of resident personal decision making. Euthanasia is legal in the Netherlands, and Humanitas will cooperate if an individual decides to follow this path and fits the regulatory constraints for doing so. They have about one case every three months.

6. The discussion of ZIN is compiled from: what Shoji Shiba learned when he visited ZIN and Wim Verschuren on the site of the Brothers of Mary, Mother of Mercy cloister in Vught in the Netherlands; an article entitled "Fraters en communicatiebedrijf starten centrum 'Zin in werk'" issue 19 of the 1999 volume of rkkerk.nl (www.katholieknederland.nl/rkkerk/media/rkkerk_gedrukt/index.html); a three-page undated document by Wim Verschuren entitled "The Movement of Mercy"; and an undated two-page memo entitled "Lessons from ZIN" drafted by Bertrand Jouslin de Noray after he visited ZIN with Shoji Shiba.

7. American Standard edition.

8. Koji Kobayashi was president and later chairman of Japan's NEC Corp. from the 1960s to the 1980s. He foresaw the convergence of computers and communications, and strongly promoted convergence as NEC's corporate mission and "C and C" (computers and communications) as

NEC's corporate slogan. To this end, he wrote books that were published as Kobayashi86 and Kobayashi91.

Chapter Nine

Initiate Transformation

This chapter addresses the second task shown in Figure 8-1—initiation of the transformation. This is a process of disrupting the existing business, putting a new mental model in place, and beginning to force change consistent with the new direction.

9.1 FAVI and Principle 3

Principle 3. Transformation is begun with *symbolic disruption* of old or traditional systems through *top-down* efforts to *create chaos* within the organization.

We saw examples of this principle in the Humanitas and ZIN case studies of Chapter 8. For instance, Humanitas stopped hiring consultants, let 20 or 30 percent of the doctors leave the organization, knocked down the traditional eldercare building, proscribed white clothes for healthcare professionals, disclosed all business results, and began to call residents "clients" instead of "patients."

When Brother Wim became the leader of his order, he went to Indonesia and closed schools and started new ones from scratch, which was a shock to the entire order. In the case of the ZIN center, he set it up so it was run by a separate company and not the order; this was a break with past practice.

The Seiko company in Japan provides a particularly dramatic example of intentional disruption of an existing organization to enable change. To enable the transformational change the company wanted to undertake, one-third of the division's people were transferred to other divisions of the company, one-third of the people were encouraged to take early retirement, and that same number of people were newly recruited into the division.

In the rest of this section, we will discuss the case study of FAVI, where we see additional examples of a visionary leader causing symbolic disruption.

Jean-François Zobrist

FAVI has 500 employees and is located in northern France, in Hallencourt, about 170 km from Paris. As shown in Figure 9-1,[1] FAVI provides a good example of the inflection point idea shown in Figure 7-3. FAVI's early business of making "sanitary siphons" that prevented sewer gases from coming into a room via a sink drain leveled off and eventually died. Today FAVI makes parts for gauges that meter water (a nongrowth business) and automobile parts, particularly shift forks (a growth business). FAVI is attempting to expand its business of making high conductivity brass rotors for electrical generators. All of FAVI's product areas over the years have related to its core technology of high-pressure die casting. FAVI's visionary leader is Jean-François Zobrist.[2]

CEO Jean-François Zobrist joined the parent company of FAVI (Fonderie et Ateliers du Vimeu), AFICA (Affinage Champagne Ardennes—Champagne Ardennes Refinery), in 1966 at the age of 21 after receiving a technical diploma (not a full college degree) and doing his military service. Over the years, he has worked in all of the functional areas of the company: the production process, development and design, process control, quality control, sales, and so on.[3]

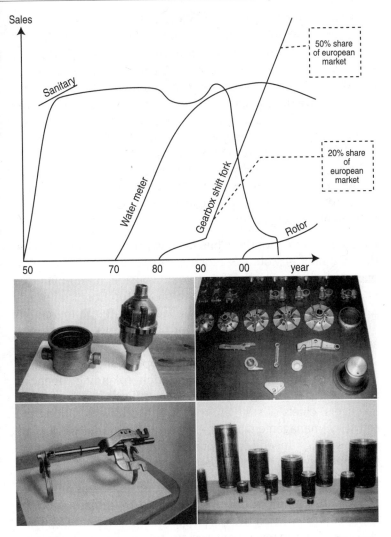

Figure 9-1. FAVI's changes of business: sanitary siphons for sink drains (top-left photo), water gauges (top right), automobile shift forks (bottom left), electrical generator rotors (bottom right)

FAVI was originally a client of AFICA, but when FAVI ran into financial trouble, AFICA bought it. Over the next years, Jean-François Zobrist dropped by FAVI from time to time as part of the effort of Max Rousseaux, CEO of AFICA, to keep an eye on things at FAVI. In the early 1980s the man running FAVI for AFICA decided to leave the company, and Jean-François Zobrist was asked by Rousseaux to find the next person to lead FAVI. But Zobrist's several suggestions of people were rejected by Rousseaux. Then, one day in April 1983, CEO Rousseaux of AFICA took Zobrist by helicopter from Reims where they worked and where Zobrist lived to FAVI in Hallencourt where the CEO called the FAVI employees together and announced (to Zobrist's great surprise) that Zobrist was the new CEO of FAVI.

For the next four months, while his predecessor remained to run the company at Zobrist's request, Zobrist observed how FAVI operated. He found what many would consider a well-managed factory (at least for then): an office on the top floor from which the CEO would observe the whole factory, careful timekeeping of hours worked (and penalties for being late), locked storage areas for consumables such as workers' gloves, a central coffee station where employees could buy a cup of coffee, a traditional hierarchical and functional organization (planning, financial, personnel, purchasing, supervisors, shop foremen, department managers, chiefs of staff, etc.), a lot of executive positions and activities (management board, executive officers' meetings, planning meetings, meetings to consider the previous month's quality problems, etc.), monthly production bonuses, and the like.

The company seemed to run well. However, because Zobrist had explicitly taken time to observe things and not taken over operational control, he had the time to think about the ramifications of the existing management system rather than just adopting it, and he began to see inefficiencies: the company lost more money in employee time than it saved by controlling the storage area and having a centralized coffee machine, the many meetings tended to work on things that were long gone by and to be a place where old scores were settled and excuses were made, the focus on accurate timekeeping was offset by employees who would queue up waiting for the end-of-day bell to ring so they could check out, and bonuses were being laboriously calculated for things the employees could not affect.

One day when Zobrist was about to mow his lawn at home, his lawn mower misfired. So he got out some tools and cleaned the spark plug, which corrected the problem; and he felt rather proud of himself for fixing the problem. Then he had an epiphany: at work, a multistep, multi-person process would have had to have been gone through to get something fixed if a worker's equipment had a problem—perhaps he could do something to just let a worker fix his own machine. FAVI's existing system, Zobrist thought, made the assumption that people were bad and needed controlling; he tried to imagine an organizational chart in which the assumption was that people were good. Not knowing quite what to do, he took some symbolic steps. For instance, he bricked up the window that allowed him to observe the whole factory from his top-floor office.

Then, around the end of the year, Zobrist called his entire staff together and announced he was implementing a people-are-good management system. He was eliminating the timekeepers, the end-of-day bell, and the lateness penalties; the goal would be to make good parts, not optimize time. He abolished the production bonuses and integrated the pay that might have come from bonuses into the normal pay rate. He unlocked the consumables stock room, and told workers to write down what they took so it could be replenished. He put free coffee stations in each workshop, so employees didn't have to take time to walk to the central paid coffee station. He also eliminated the regular managers' and planning meetings. In our terms, Zobrist had clearly applied

Principle 3: from the top, he made symbolic disruptions that initially risked (at least emotional) chaos within the organization.

CEO Zobrist had an explicit image of what sort of company FAVI should be. According to him, FAVI's goal was to continue to *durer* (to last) in its town in France by working intimately with its customers to continually adapt to current customer needs, and he adopted the tree for his symbol of the company (see Figure 9-2). He asked rhetorically, "Does a tree want to be number one or the best?" No a tree just wants to *durer*—to last. The objective of FAVI is the same—just *durer* in the small village of Hallencourt. Zobrist's next rhetorical logic was:

> What do people need to *durer*? Please close your mouth, hold your nose, and stop breathing.... I hope you understand what is necessary for humans to *durer*. They need air.

> Air is necessary for humans to *durer*. What is necessary for FAVI to *durer*? The answer is money. We French tend to think that money is not decent. But we need money for *durer*.

> How do we get money? Good quality of products is not enough. L'*amour* from each customer is necessary to get money.

Dramatically, Zobrist compared what FAVI needed to do to a street walker: she has to look attractive to her customers and she wears a little makeup to be noticed (FAVI will be clean and painted in bright colors), she specializes in something customers want (FAVI will make the best possible pieces of rough cast metal), and she doesn't give her customers illness (FAVI will have no delivery delays and produce nothing with poor quality). Finally, there was the question of what price to set for their services; Zobrist stated they would never raise their prices again, so that one day they would have the best prices in France or perhaps the world.

Figure 9-2. Top: Jean-François Zobrist and a symbolic tree; Bottom: Trees are symbols on the FAVI campus

Later, Zobrist had the problem that the person leading the machining department couldn't manage the department as it grew in size. Rather than just change managers, FAVI set up a minifactory for each specific customer. This solved the management problem and created *l'amour*—to have an intimate relationship with the particular customer.

Jean-François Zobrist likes to show the illustration reproduced in Figure 9-3. The figure caption gives his explanation for this figure.

In describing this, Zobrist makes it clear (as was explicit with the street walker example) that he includes the sexual connotation of *l'amour* in his view of the metaphorical love relationship with the customer. FAVI and the customer work together from conception—R&D as well as design and production of products for the customer.

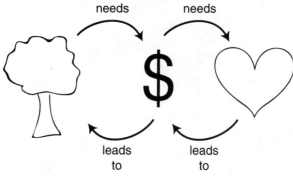

Figure 9-3. To durer in place like a tree requires money and that, in turn, requires being loved intimately by a single customer. Doing what it takes to be loved intimately by one customer leads to dollars which lead to being able to be like a tree and stay in one place.

FAVI's management system

The new system of management used by FAVI flows from the CEO's *beliefs*, as shown at the top of Figure 9-4, Shoji Shiba's partial model of FAVI's management system.

At the top of the model, we see that CEO Zobrist believes "man is good," that is, freedom from control. The company eliminated procedures for attendance (i.e., time clocks), stopped the premium system (i.e., piecework payment), and encouraged open discussion of all business information. In other words, the CEO decided to trust the employees—he moved from a Theory X approach to a Theory Y approach to management.

Zobrist's philosophy of management of assuming man is good

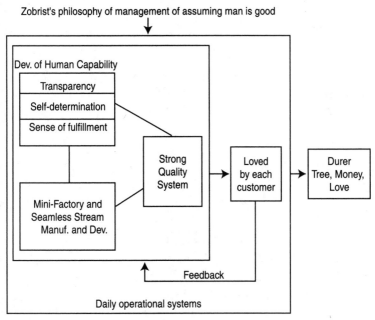

Figure 9-4. Model of the FAVI *management system*

Once upon a time, workers thought of work in terms of doing their job in the specified way. (We call this "product-out.") More recently the pressure of competition and rapid change required the concept of work to evolve to be "satisfying customers." (We called this "market-in."[4]) In the FAVI case, we see a further evolution of the concept of work. When freedom and trust are considered in the context of CEO Zobrist's analogy in Figure 9-3—to exist in place like a tree requires money and that, in turn, requires being loved intimately by a single customer—it leads to a new *concept of work*. The new concept of work relates to a specific customer rather than customers in general and it involves the situations of the workers (continuing to exist in their town); in other words, the new concept of work combines more-specific versions of product-out and market-in in a win-win situation for workers and customers.

FAVI's *operation system* is shown near the lower middle of Figure 9-4. The operation system has two major components.

First, FAVI has *mini-factories* dedicated to particular customers, as shown in Figure 9-5. There may be more than one mini-factory for a particular customer, as shown in the figure. About 20 such mini-factories exist.

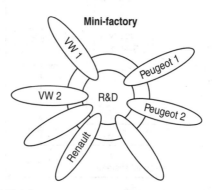

Figure 9-5. *Multiple mini-factories*

A mini-factory is a production facility with a set of equipment, and with a leader and perhaps 20 other people. The leader functions as a mini-CEO with responsibility for getting the next job from the customer.

Each mini-factory has its own goals, for instance, relating to production plans, for human resources, and for investing in training and other methods of increasing productivity.

Second, FAVI has *seamless integration* from R&D through sales, manufacturing, and post-sale follow-up. In the same building work a strong R&D group consisting of 30 people covering two shifts, the mini-factory and its leader, and a 15-person customer relations group from which one person provides liaison to the customer of the mini-factory.

Near the top middle of Figure 9-4 the *human system* is shown, aimed at maximizing employee motivation. It is based on principles of self-direction, transparency, and feeling effective. The mini-factories are a version of self-directed work teams, where the team is empowered to plan production and take action to increase the skills of the team and its members (including providing a single employee with skill in more than one area). The transparency includes the already mentioned openness with financial figures (such as sales and profits) aimed at increasing trust within the organization. There are also bonuses awarded at four- to five- month intervals. The feeling of effectiveness—gratification for a job well done—is fostered through intense training (10–12 percent of FAVI's personnel costs vs. a French average of 2 percent) and outside visits including to other countries such as Japan and Poland.

Regarding the *quality management system* (bottom of Figure 9-4), in 1983 FAVI was the first company in France to introduce the 5S method. In 1987, FAVI was the first company in France to introduce Total Productive Maintenance (TPM). In 2002, FAVI became the first company in France to be certified in ISO 9001:2000, QS9000, FAQF ISO 14001, and OHSAS 18001.

Feedback is implicit in the parts of the FAVI management system we have already described. The customer-specific mini-factories, the R&D department responsiveness to customers, and the customer relations person who interacts between a customer and the mini-factory and R&D department all provide strong feedback paths.

9.2 SOL and Principle 4

Principle 4. The direction of transformation is illustrated aimed by a symbolic *visible image* and the visionary leader's *symbolic behavior*.

Humanitas (Chapter 8) provided a giant physical "visualized direction" through the construction of its first mixed use building complex, with apartments for healthy as well as ill residents and retail businesses that made the complex into its own little village integrated with the surrounding town. The building complex clearly showed Humanitas' aim to provide an attractive and lively home for life for the elderly people who came there to live.

At ZIN the visualized direction is much more of a spiritual and long-term symbol. ZIN's goal was to continue its historical, spiritual mission of mercy. Collocating the new facilities with the cemetery where the Brothers of Mercy had been buried for more than 150 years and with the church with the painting of the Five Styles of Mercy clearly indicated the direction in which ZIN intended to keep going, albeit with somewhat modern means.

At FAVI Jean-François Zobrist summarizes his philosophy in one small illustration (Figure 9-3) and with vivid language about intimacy with customers.

SOL and Liisa Joronen

SOL is a family-owned, Finnish service company. It provides laundry services to consumers and to other businesses, and it provides a variety of facility services including contract cleaning and janitorial services, building maintenance, and various specialized services from gardening to reception services. The company has 7,200 employees, a large number of whom are hourly employees. The company's 2005 revenue (turnover) was 118 million euros.[5]

The roots of SOL go back to the early 1900s when SOL CEO Liisa Joronen's grandfather bought a small dyeing, laundry, and dry cleaning business, named Lindstrom, in Helsinki. Joronen's father expanded the business to include textile rental and then office cleaning. Ms. Joronen always intended to participate in the Lindstrom company, and in 1981 she was appointed managing director. But Ms. Joronen's innovative ideas for how the company should be managed clashed with the more-traditional management ideas of other members of her family; thus, in 1991, Ms. Joronen's father split the company in two parts with her taking the (at the time, not profitable) cleaning business while her brother and sisters took the laundry and linen rental business.

Freedom is important in Finnish culture. In particular, freedom is a key aspect of the personal philosophy of SOL CEO Liisa Joronen and, thus, an important aspect of the SOL company culture. SOL boasts:

▶ Freedom from the workplace

▶ Freedom from working hours

▶ Freedom from status symbols

SOL employees often work from home. There are no fixed desks at the head office—there are employees in the head office but not as many places to sit as there are employees. Work shifts are available any time of the day or night and any day of the year. CEO Joronen herself doesn't have a private office, car, or secretary.

When SOL was launched on its own, with more enthusiasm than finances, the studio space of a bankrupt movie company was rented, and the early employees contributed numerous suggestions about what the office environment should be like. In particular, they decided it should be less like an office and more like an imaginary home. A unique office design resulted that immediately showed (Principle 4) something different was happening at SOL to both clients and employees, as did CEO Joronen's eschewing executive perks.

CEO Joronen says, "SOL City, our head office (Figure 9-6), is a symbol of our corporate culture. Our corporate culture is freedom." As shown in the top-left photo, SOL City is free of a standard office style. As shown in the top-right photo, seating is quite untraditional—no traditional desks and no private offices. Also shown in that photo (lower right corner) is a long black piece of furniture that contains lots of "cubbies"—like in kindergarten class—for employees to store their belongings in. In the bottom left of Figure 9-6 we see CEO Joronen who came in late and has found a place to sit in the company kitchen. The other offices of SOL are also conceived by the local employees with the only rule being that they have to reflect the company's philosophy of "freedom, responsibility, trust, creativity, happiness at work, and learning throughout life." [6]

When employees visit customers, they wear uniforms (Figure 9-6, bottom right) that are very bright—like the sun (sol). SOL thinks of itself as "the sunny company." (See http://www.sol.fi/.) Ms. Joronen herself always wears yellow in both business and private life.

Based on his visit and study of SOL, Shoji Shiba sees the model shown in Figure 9-7 for how SOL manages as a company.

The *operation system* of SOL—how the company's business is carried out—is based on small enterprises—"self-directed work groups" of up to 10 people. There are hundreds of these small enterprises.

The small enterprises have the freedom to change their approach or style of work to adapt to customer needs. They also have freedom to invest enterprise resources in obtaining manpower and new skills.

There is no company-wide target. Rather, each small enterprise sets its own five targets. The small enterprise targets include:

▸ Total sales per year

▸ Customer satisfaction (on the laugh and smile scale shown below)

◗ Profit

◗ Investment in training and education

◗ A diagnostic score, rated by a company team

Figure 9-6. SOL City and SOL culture

Each small enterprise also has responsibility for participating in two "SOL Days" in January and two in August. During these days, the hundreds of team leaders present their targets and results and decide on their challenges for the next period of time.

The SOL *human system* is also based on the self-directed work groups. Furthermore, all business information is open to all employees except personnel data. The goal of the human system is *human development*, not profit. The assumption is that personal gratification comes from self-fulfillment: from development as a human being, and from making the customer happy.

As already alluded to, SOL doesn't use company targets. However, without a company target, something else is needed to align activities throughout the company. For such alignment, in place of company targets, SOL employees actively empathize with customers and obtain direct *feedback* from customers. SOL people think they are part of the customer's business and the customer is a part of SOL.

At SOL, the self-directed work groups with five to 10 members and a leader regularly seek five types of customer feedback:

1. Monthly feedback

2. Direct, anonymous feedback from customers

3. Customer surveys by a third party

4. Surveys of unhappy customers (for example, customers who have left)

5. Diagnosis of the feedback system itself

There are two kinds of monthly feedback: face-to-face questioning of the customers by the service worker (using a standard format of questions) and a monthly interview of the group leader by the area manager. The latter covers the gap between expectation and results, opportunities for improvement, a review of past commit-

Joronen's philosophy of growth of the human being

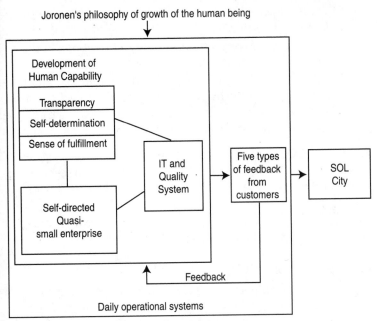

Figure 9-7. *Model of the* SOL *management system*

ments and results, the most important concern of the customer, and a overall evaluation on a laugh, smile, ..., frown scale (see Figure 9-8), which are actually percentage metrics.

Figure 9-8. *Customer evaluation scale*

It is CEO Liisa Joronen's *belief* that the job of the CEO is to transform the mental setting within the company from being based on control to being based on full *trust* of the people and the resultant freedom for the people. This is why no overall company target is used (CEO Joronen sees company targets as containing a hint of mistrust) and why self-directed work groups are used. Liisa Joronen views SOL City as a symbol of this freedom and the trust that is required to support the freedom.

Finally, the SOL management system depends on a *quality and IT system*. On the IT side of things, the company is 98 percent paperless. On the quality side of things, SOL won the 1993 National Quality Award in Finland. Previously, in 1991, the parent company had won the Finnish National Quality Award. (The parent company introduced a quality system in 1979.)

Making the goal visible

In essence, Principle 4 involves two activities: making the goal visible and showing symbolic behavior. This and the next subsection consider some specific approaches to these two activities.

First, we recommend a hierarchy of goals: a) noble goals such as "better living through chemistry" or "benefit to customers" that are unchanging for many years into the future; b) intermediate goals that extend three or four years into the future such as "improve development process," "achieving Six Sigma," or Teradyne's "market share up, cost down, and cycle time down"; c) and typical annual operational goals [Shiba93, pp. 339–340].

Intermediate goals are the most relevant of the goal hierarchy to breakthrough. They are mental images or models of what the company should look like. In addition to stating the objective, there are two other aspects of intermediate goals: providing an image of success, and encouraging behavior favorable to achieving the goal.

Some example success images are President Kennedy's image of the United States putting a man on the moon within the decade, RCA Sarnoff Research Lab's desire to develop a TV that hung on the wall, or Shuji Nakamura's dream of creating a blue color laser-emitting diode. Such success images play an important role in motivating people toward the desired breakthrough.

We all know about the success of the U.S. man-on-the-moon program. At Sarnoff Lab, the expressed desire to develop a TV that hung on the wall motivated much, highly focused research. Shuji Nakamura focused his thinking on the color blue, the colors of light more generally, and the idea that if one could get another color LED, shouldn't he be able to change the materials to get another color?

An example of encouraging behavior favorable to achieving the goal comes from NEC's Semiconductor Division that was trying to achieve customer satisfaction and high performance. The division's intermediate goal was to get a "half-step ahead" of its competitors and included components of "visiting on site 100 times" and "face-to-face communication."

Another example, in effect, of a subgoal for encouraging behavior favorable to achieving a larger goal is found in a quote by Dave Clark of MIT at the Internet Engineering Task Force's 1992 meeting: "We reject: kings, presidents, and voting. We believe in: rough consensus and running code." Known informally as the IETF Credo, this means don't do things based on authority or popularity; do things because enough people are in agreement and they have something that works.[7] For a long time, the approach described in the credo allowed the Internet to develop without the sort of politically motivated system designs and unhealthy or overly complex compromises that have come out of some international standards creation efforts in the computer and communications arena.

Intermediate goals must be described in *words*. Use both affective and objective language. Use affective words to clearly and simply state the goal in an easy-to-remember way. Use objective or logical words to attractively and innovatively capture the essence of what is desired and to focus attention on it.

Here are some tips for creating an effective goal statement:

1. Use behavioral words that indicate what to do going forward.

2. Fit the words to human nature.

3. Use the ladder of abstraction effectively.

The IETF Credo includes behavioral words such as "reject" and "believe." President Kennedy's human-on-the-moon speech included behavioral words such as "choose to go" and "unwilling to postpone." There is a long tradition of use of such "to be" and "not to be" behavioral words to help aim a company; we remember that Alfred Sloan stated his goals for General Motors in terms of "GM always does" and "GM never does." [8]

Fitting the words to human nature means making them easy to remember—short with a small number of items to remember. For instance, Teradyne used MC^2 (Marketshare up, Cost down, Cycle-time down) as the intermediate goal for its push to implement Total Quality Management techniques. (Remember the efficiency of a three-legged stool—two legs are unstable while a fourth leg is redundant.) The words also have to be well fit to the corporate culture. For instance, during a 2001 visit to Dell, Shoji Shiba heard the slogan "Kill Compaq"; this was consistent with the aggressive Dell corporate culture, and by 2002 Dell had surpassed Compaq. Finally, repetition of the words is important if humans are expected to remember them. Think of President Lincoln's "government of the people, by the people, for the people," or Mohandas Gandhi's "One's faith in one's plans and methods is truly tested when the horizon before one is the blackest" [Gandhi97], or Martin Luther King's "I have a dream..."

An example of effectively using the ladder of abstraction comes from a presentation at a JUSE conference near Tokyo in 1998 by Hajime Sasaki of NEC's Semiconductor Division. His intermediate goal statement included three components: 1) half-step ahead, 2) visit sites 100 times, and 3) face-to-face communication. Each of these three components was positioned on the ladder of abstraction between a more-abstract term and a more-specific statement (see Figure 9-9). For instance, "half-step ahead" is the "operational principle" component of Mr. Sasaki's intermediate goal, and "all business activities must move a half-step ahead of competitors to meet market/customer needs" is a more-detailed statement of what "half-step ahead" means.

1.	Operational principle **Half-step ahead** All business activity must move a half-step ahead of competitors to meet market/customer needs
2.	Action principle **Visit sites 100 times** Basics of business activity exist on site
3.	Organizational principle **Face-to-face communication** All business activity will be done through direct face-to-face discussion

Figure 9-9. Effective use of ladder of abstraction

Symbolic behavior

It is not sufficient to "talk the talk" about the new direction of the business and ways it will operate. A visionary leader must also "walk the talk" by serving as a role model for the desired change. Any deviation between the leader's actions and decisions and the leader's pronouncements will be viewed with great cynicism by the employees of the business. As Frank Pipp (onetime director of manufacturing and R&D at Xerox) said, "Employees can smell management hypocrisy at three parts in a million."

The leader is always being watched

The leader's actions are an ongoing source of symbolic behavior. Even if the leader does not intend to be performing a symbolic act (or any significant act at all), the people watching may well read symbolic significance into the act (or lack of action). Thus, a leader must not show lack of integrity—always there must be consistency between the leader's words and actions.

Since the leader is always being watched, this is a potential source of power. The leader can show the desired strategic direction by presenting him- or herself as a role model. Recognizing the symbolic nature of his or her action, the leader should use these symbolic actions to amplify the mechanisms of change within the organization.

Of course, various leaders (obviously not all) have known about the importance of providing a role model "forever." For instance, the Medici family of Italy in the 1500s knew of the importance of being seen by the public as part of the source of their power. When the Medici family built a theater in Florence, Italy, they included a space for themselves at the center of the theater—where the public could see their behavior and power at public events held in the theater.

U.S. examples from the last couple of decades include the Malcolm Baldrige National Quality Awards where the CEOs crusaded throughout the U.S., diffusing the message of quality to the U.S. As part of the founding of the Center for Quality of Management[9] in 1990, the top managers of CQM-founding companies presented a symbolic role model by being the first people from their companies to attend CQM's "six-day course" and (as shown in the photographs of Figure 9-10) working at the class exercises as any less-senior employee would.

Figure 9-10. Executives in CQM six-day course

Symbolic behavior is the key

In 1990, when Alex d'Arbeloff was leading the introduction of TQM into Teradyne, Teradyne held TQM seminars for all its employees, taught by Shoji Shiba. Shoji Shiba gave homework assignments as part of his teaching. CEO d'Arbeloff would come 30 minutes before class started to post his homework assignment in a central location on the wall of the seminar room. The other executives and managers followed Alex's model and posted their homework.

Another example of symbolic behavior comes from Louis Gerstner's *Who Says Elephants Can't Dance?*, in a subsection of the book entitled "The Click Heard Round the World" [Gerstner03, p. 43] where he describes an early meeting he called to learn the state of the business. Gerstner says:

> At that time, the standard format of any important IBM meeting was a presentation using overhead projectors and graphics on transparencies that IBMers called—and no one remembers why—"foils." Nick was on his second foil when I stepped to the table and, as politely as I could in front of his team, switched off the project. After a long moment of awkward silence, I simply said, "Let's just talk about your business."
>
> I mention this episode because it had an unintended, but terribly powerful, ripple effect. By the afternoon an e-mail about my hitting the Off button on the overhead projector was crisscrossing the world. Talk about consternation! It was as if the President of the United States had banned the use of English at White House meetings.

Still another example of symbolic behavior comes from Mr. Shoichiro Toyoda in December of 1998. At a three-day JUSE[10] conference at a hotel in Hakone (a mountain resort area some ways from Tokyo), the Toyota Quality Division had organized the conference speakers. Mr. Toyoda was to be the keynote speaker. But the president of Argentina unexpectedly scheduled a visit to the Toyota factory; and, one day before he was to speak, Mr. Toyoda had to cancel his keynote presentation in order to host the visit of the president of Argentina. However, at 11 p.m. in the evening, Mr. Toyoda arrived, through snow, at the conference hotel, a significant distance from the Toyota factory, and he apologized to all the conference participants for having had to cancel his keynote address. This symbolic gesture had considerable impact on the conference participants and reemphasized Mr. Toyoda's strong commitment to quality.

In a recent example symbolizing his commitment to quality, Mr. Toyoda personally attended the Deming Prize ceremony of Mr. Akira Takahashi who won the individual Deming Prize on November 9, 2004.

The leader must use the effective methods available

In his book, *Only the Paranoid Survive*, Andy Grove notes three areas in which a leader can affect his organization:

▶ Promoting or replacing people, e.g., over a few years perhaps half of the executives might be changed

▶ Allocation of resources, e.g., opening new branch offices or closing existing branch offices, starting a new production line, etc.

▶ Use of the leader's personal time, e.g., what the leader attends or doesn't attend, how much time the leader allocates to his or her own learning, etc.

Andy Grove says that if you do not change the executives, you cannot change anything. When Teradyne established its TQM program, CEO Alex d'Arbeloff moved one of his most promising young managers from heading the U.S. sales force to the staff position of corporate quality officer. In about 18 months, this manager was rotated back into a high-level line management role, and another promising young manager was named corporate quality officer. Over a decade, Teradyne filled its top management ranks with people who had once served as corporate quality officer and, thus, firmly changed the management view to one where quality and the methods of producing quality were part of the corporate culture. Later, for Teradyne's Aurora project [Shiba01], d'Arbeloff selected one of his most valuable and respected engineers to lead the project. In addition to using managers who would help change the corporate culture and practice, such personnel assignments also show how serious d'Arbeloff was about what he was trying to accomplish.

Also for Teradyne's Aurora project, Alex d'Arbeloff showed his determination to start a new product line by placing the new activity in a location apart from Teradyne's existing factory.

The symbolic value of redeployment of the leader's personal time is of incalculable value—how the leader spends his or her time is closely watched by the rest of the company, and actions speak louder than words. The leader's calendar can become his or her most important strategic tool. Alex d'Arbeloff suggests that a CEO should spend 20 percent of his or her time creating something completely new, and he always allocated this percentage of his time to new activities—introducing TQM in 1990, starting the Aurora project in 1993, and so on.

A leader needs to have appropriate character

A leader must illustrate consistency and integrity. The leader should:

- Avoid ambiguity

- Not hedge risks

- Not go around in circles

The leader needs to show consistency of thought, word, and behavior, with each other and over time.

A leader needs to be open to learning new things. For instance, Ray Stata, founder of Analog Devices and cofounder of the Center for Quality of Management (CQM), was a motivating force in learning about TQM, studying the methods of conversation, and studying the methods of leadership.

A leader who is a role model also needs to show control of him- or herself. Such control can range from not losing his or her temper or panicking to not writing nasty memos to keeping physically fit to doing something hard and lonely. If the leader cannot control him- or herself, it will be difficult for the followers to accept the leader, and the leader will not be able to lead.

It's not sufficient just to have integrity of thoughts, words, and deeds at work. You can't pretend at work and be someone else outside of work. Essential to being a highly effective role model is for the leader to unite his or her way of life with the management direction he or she desires.

9.3 Principle 5

Principle 5. Quickly establishing new *physical*, *organizational*, and *behavioral systems* is essential for successful transformation.

We saw examples of the application of this principle in the Humanitas and ZIN case studies of Chapter 8 and the FAVI and SOL case studies of this chapter. For example, Humanitas made the physical change of building a new mixed use building, FAVI made the organizational change of establishing mini-factories to better enable intimate relationships with customers, and at SOL everyone shared a common office space. Table 9-1 summarizes some of the physical, organizational, and behavioral changes at Humanitas, ZIN, FAVI, and SOL.

Table 9-1. *Principle 5 at Humanitas, ZIN, FAVI, and SOL*

	Physical	Organizational	Behavioral
Humanitas	New mixed use building	Involving the extended family Moving from care to housing	Use it or lose it philosophy Yes culture
ZIN	New building combined with old church	Seeing, being moved, and then taking action	To love themselves
FAVI	Mini-factories	Close relationship with customers Uniting R&D and manufacturing	Trust by the CEO
SOL	SOL City	Intensive feedback from customers	Self-directed work teams Trust by the CEO

Common language

The physical and organizational changes a visionary leader makes are likely to be very situational, as are the behavioral changes. However, one kind of behavioral change is very often useful and all too often not utilized; this is the use of common language.

When trying to carry out change in an organization, experience has shown that efforts to promote a common language to talk about the change can help make the change. For instance, in companies that were not focused on customers, beginning to use the words "customer focus" naturally lead to most people becoming more aware of the fact that they have customers (even internal customers) and that customers have needs. Moving toward the innovative goal that is inherent in a breakthrough effort causes a disconnect with the existing corporate culture, and efforts to spread a new set of words—a new common language—throughout the organization can help bridge the gap of the disconnect.

The American best-selling book *Who Moved My Cheese?* [Johnson98] was translated into Japanese; and, from November 2000 through January 2001, 900,000 copies (roughly 15,000 copies per business day) of the book were sold. The concept and the language of this book by Spencer Johnson are that change always happens, don't fear it, individuals must adapt to change as soon as possible, changing past behavior and moving in the direction of the change; the book creates a vision of change. A large part of the reason this 94-page parable of change sold so many copies in Japan was because companies distributed the book to employees to provide a common language of change. (A longtime best-seller in the U.S., the book has been used in many U.S. companies and other institutions.)

Adopting a common language for talking about change is so powerful because it helps in several ways. First, learning new vocabulary lets people see what they didn't see before, as in the example of not thinking about having customers until one begins to talk about "customers," at which time it becomes obvious that the next process in a series of manufacturing processes is the customer of the previous step.

Next, a common language helps bridge the cultural differences within an organization and thus creates a readiness for transformation. For instance, in a multinational company, different countries may have different national or business cultures that seem unique (and may well be), but this uniqueness may also be used as an excuse: "We are unique and thus the parent company's goals don't apply to us and we can't change." There are also cultural differences among functional areas of a company that can be as different as national differences. For instance, the accounting people naturally think in terms of profitability and breakeven points and live in a world where it is assumed that providing a return on investment is the paramount goal of the business. On the other hand, the research and development people naturally think in terms of creativity and innovation and live in a world where it is assumed that providing the next technology breakthrough is of paramount importance.

Adopting a common language of "interacting causal loops" could help both functions see how they fit together to achieve the goals of the overall organization.

The common language also can be couched in a way that diffuses the desired direction of change and goals. For instance, Humanitas talks about the "yes culture"; this helps employees remember to be responsive to clients as well as to be willing to think innovatively.

Finally, the common language can be publicized as part of the branding of the organization. The "yes culture" of Humanitas is prominently mentioned in Humanitas' marketing materials.

Training and education activities have long been used to convey a common language to people in a company. For instance, training of quality control circles in Japan starting in the early 1960s conveyed a common language of "plan-do-check-act," "QC stories" (7 steps), and "market-in/product-out" throughout companies and across industries in Japan. More recently, in 1987 in Hungary, there was a desire to introduce Total Quality Management to industry as part of improving the country's planned economy. However, at the time they had no word for "management" in general—only words like "operation," "manipulation," and "control." Therefore, the training in TQM used the English word for "management," and that provided a new element of common language across industry that helped spread the desired changes.

In addition to training, one can simply use repetition to help create a common language. Every time the leader speaks, he or she can repeat a key phrase, such as "yes culture" at Humanitas. The outside-in communication technique can also be used to bring the desired common language to a business, as we believe Andy Grove brought a sense of urgency to Intel through publication of his book, *Only the Paranoid Survive*.

9.4 Reflection

The CEO philosophies and management systems of SOL (section 9.2) and FAVI (section 9.1) have certain similarities, starting with a new work concept illustrated in a symbolic way (SOL City and FAVI's tree) and continuing with similar models of management.

Also, in both the SOL and FAVI cases, the CEO works from the border of the organization, where she or he can work equally well either inside or outside the organization, rather than centered at the top of the traditional hierarchical organization. CEO Zobrist suggests that a CEO should be like a football coach—not in the middle of the field but standing at the sidelines where he can see signals for change both inside and outside of the team. CEO Zobrist works to spend 20 percent of his time outside the organization, including outside conferences a couple of times a month and an outside meeting once a week.

In both cases the CEO also works up and down the ladder of abstraction, from the conceptual to the concrete level, in reaction to seeing signals for change.[11] Both CEOs grapple conceptually with defining the real objective of the organization—a what-does-life-mean sort of question. At the concrete level, FAVI implemented the 5S method and SOL has a process for going to the customer to fix the problem.

There are also some contrasts between the ways SOL and FAVI handle things. SOL meets directly with customers while the connection to customers at FAVI is through the customer relations person. SOL addresses change with specific improvements in the workplace while FAVI concentrates on rapid technical change.

Figure 9-11 relates what we covered in this chapter with what we covered in the previous chapter (see Figure 8-6) and points to where we are going in the next chapter.

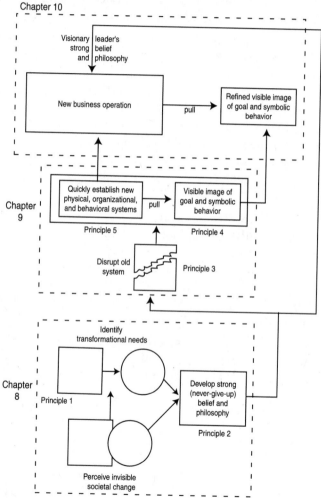

Figure 9-11. *Principles 3–5 in context*

As we saw in this chapter in the FAVI and SOL case studies, the visionary leaders of those businesses used the vision and commitment they developed applying Principles 1 and 2 to initiate change. The case studies of FAVI and SOL also described the new business systems that FAVI and SOL's leaders created, and we will return to a model for what they did in the next chapter.

Because of the way we built up the presentation of the principles and case studies in the previous chapter and this chapter, we have not yet highlighted the application of some of Principles 1–5 in some of the case studies. A complete set of summary charts are included at the end of Chapter 10.

Notes

1. Created by French quality expert Martine Morel.

2. Shoji Shiba first heard of FAVI at an EOQ summer camp in 2001. In 2002, Shoji Shiba visited FAVI in Hallencourt for a day and talked with CEO Jean-François Zobrist. In 2004, Jean Lefebvre, a professor of international management at the University of Connecticut and a French speaker, visited FAVI for two days, and Shiba and Lefebvre have written a paper [Lefebvre06] describing FAVI and analyzing FAVI's management system. Jean-François Zobrist has also been interviewed by Elisabeth Ballery (included in section 1 of this book). We also read a three-page document about "FAVI's Breakthrough" prepared by Martine Morel. Our description and understanding of FAVI comes from these sources.

3. This and the next four paragraphs are derived from Elisabeth Ballery's interview.

4. Product-out and market-in are explained in detail in Shiba01.

5. Shoji Shiba heard a presentation by Liisa Joronen, the CEO of SOL, at the European Organization for Quality 2001 "summer camp." In October of 2002, Shoji Shiba visited SOL and talked with CEO Joronen. Liisa Joronen has also been interviewed by Elisabeth Ballery (included in section 1 of this book). Our description and understanding of SOL comes from these sources.

6. From the Ballery interview.

7. We can't remember if this is our interpretation or if we heard it from someone else.

8. Unfortunately, we cannot remember the appropriate citation for this.

9. www.cqm.org.

10. Japanese Union of Scientists and Engineers, perhaps Japan's most significant quality organization.

11. CEO Liisa Joronen wrote her Ph.D. thesis on internal rewards.

Chapter Ten

Build
New Business

This chapter addresses the third task shown in Figure 8-1—creation of a new business process. This is a process of implementing a new organization and systems and the tools for these new business structures to be improved over time.

10.1 Maeda Corporation and Principle 6

Principle 6. *Real change leaders* are necessary to enable transformation.

The CEO alone cannot achieve a breakthrough. There must also be people who help the CEO diffuse the desired change throughout the organization, even without the CEO being present on some occasions.

Matabee Maeda and Kazuie Yamada

The case study of the Maeda Corporation provides a particularly good example of the visionary leader, Dr. Maeda, involving a real change leader, Dr. Yamada.

At the time we are describing, Dr. Matabee Maeda was the owner, chairman, and CEO of Maeda Corporation. He does not have a technical background; rather, he is a liberal arts graduate.[1]

Circa November 1989, Maeda Corporation had a project to construct a skyscraper residential building in Sapporo. Sapporo is a cold place in winter, and mixing, pouring, and setting high strength concrete is more difficult when it is cold. The Maeda Corp. engineers and concrete experts succeeded in conquering the problems and, on the day of the company's annual anniversary celebration and over drinks, proudly described the problems with the Sapporo project and their successful effort to Dr. Maeda. Part of the problem has to do with getting the compounds and water in the concrete to mix well in cold weather. Dr. Maeda, who makes Japanese noodles as a hobby, asked the engineers if it would help to mix the concrete the way dough is mixed for Japanese noodles, but the engineers didn't think his idea was relevant to concrete. Later, at the senior executive board meeting, Dr. Maeda saw a video about a newly developed high performance concrete known as self-compacting concrete; this concrete had revolutionary performance but requires more careful mixing than conventional concrete. Again, Dr. Maeda wondered if the mixing method used for Japanese noodle dough might be applied.

Dr. Maeda likes to serve guests noodles he has made himself (Figure 10-1). Noodle-making technique involves mixing the dough and rolling it in certain ways. Regarding noodles and concrete, he thought:

> Excellent noodles come from excellent technique of kneading. Japanese noodle experts have applied their genius to developing masterful techniques of mixing. In our business of construction, concrete requires mixing. But the principle used in concrete mixing is limited to stirring; it does not involve a kneading action. The kneading technique used in making noodles in Japan since long ago can be applied to mixing concrete.

Figure 10-1. *Dr. Maeda (left) practicing his noodle-making hobby and Dr. Yamada*

The noodle-making process involves a series of rolling in one direction, folding in half, rolling in the other direction, etc., as shown in Figure 10-2. No stirring is involved once the components of the dough have been initially mixed together.

With strong support from only one other person, Dr. Kazuie Yamada, Dr. Maeda had a prototype concrete mixing machine built. (Dr. Maeda and Dr. Yamada are pictured in Figure 10-1.) This machine (A in Figure 10-3) showed good potential to Dr. Maeda.

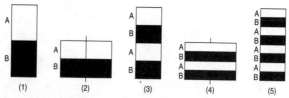

Figure 10-2. Japanese noodle kneading

Next, Dr. Maeda thought he saw an opportunity for a joint project with two other companies to develop an operational machine. However, the prototypes they attempted to build failed, and they met strong resistance, especially from experts in concrete technology, i.e., people with Ph.D.s in concrete material. They all tried to persuade Dr. Maeda not to develop a noodle-type concrete mixing machine.

Dr. Maeda described the resistance as follows:

> When I proposed using noodle-mixing techniques to mix concrete, almost all the experts in my company laughed off my idea. This was the start of a long and difficult journey that exposed me to considerable scorn and derision. At the time I was president. The project was characterized as the president's folly. However, my rebellious spirit never weakened.

Dr. Maeda did not give up even in the face of strong resistance. He was determined to go on without external partners. He did a laboratory experiment that appeared to work, and he demanded that an internal team be created to work on the problem. Dr. Kazuie Yamada was on the team as were three others who were against undertaking the effort. Led by Dr. Yamada, they built a series of prototypes (Figure 10-3), even though some of them didn't work. Finally, they developed a new type of mixer and focused on actual use on construction sites with "development partners"; this resulted in developing an operational concrete mixing machine using the Japanese noodle principle. The final machine is in practical use and is known an M-Y Mixer (for Maeda-Yamada

Mixer). In recognition of his innovation and his extraordinary documentation of the process of innovation, Dr. Maeda was awarded a doctorate in engineering from the University of Tokyo.

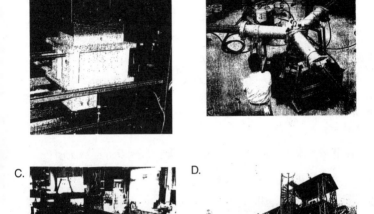

Figure 10-3. *Series of concrete mixing machines using Japanese noodle-kneading principle*

Dr. Maeda's work did not stop after the several development iterations that finally led to a working mixer that used the Japanese noodle principle. His next goal was to diffuse the new mixing technology for other uses, such as clay mixing or even noodle mixing. Each business sector will undoubtedly have its own resistance to such disruptive technology; for instance, the Japanese noodle industry is committed to the traditional hand-mixing method.

Dr. Maeda summarizes, "Decisions in organizations tend to place their emphasis on feasibility—possibility of realization. But there is no breakthrough if you just fulfill what seems feasible." Dr. Maeda suggests that a young engineer could never develop a good idea like the Japanese-noodle-principle concrete mixing machine in the face of organizational resistance. Even Dr. Maeda as chairman could barely push the idea through. Consequently, he established a small, informal school within the Maeda Corporation to develop the innovative ideas of young employees that the organization would typically kill. He calls this the "Maeda incubator of venture business."

Real change leaders

Following Katzenbach [Katzenbach95], we use the term "real change leaders" for people like Dr. Yamada who make the implementation happen, so it does not just remain another wild idea of the visionary leader.

Katzenbach describes *seven characteristics of real change leaders*:

1. Commitment to a better way

2. Courage to challenge existing power bases and norms

3. Personal initiative to go beyond defined boundaries

4. Motivation of themselves and others

5. Caring about how people are treated and enabled to perform

6. Staying undercover

7. A sense of humor about themselves and their situations

We only hinted at Dr. Yamada's role as real change leader in the Maeda case study where CEO Maeda has Dr. Yamada to face the disagreement of the rest of the organization and to actually solve many of the technical problems [Maeda02]. In fact, while Dr. Maeda had the mental breakthrough of imagining a new way of mixing concrete based on his hobby of making Japanese noodles, Dr. Yamada had the mental breakthrough that led to a practical implementation of noodle dough folding using industrial-size concrete mixing equipment. Although this part of the story is not told in the paper just cited, the mental breakthrough that allowed noodle-like folding as a concrete mixing process was geometric in nature. As can be seen in the schematic diagram in Figure 10-4, partially mixed concrete falling into the two openings at one end of the component is rotated 90 degrees by the time it comes out the other end of the box. Although we won't go through the details of demonstrating it here, a sequence of several of the units shown in Figure 10-4 with each unit rotating the concrete going through it plus or minus 90 degrees allows "folding" of the concrete similar to the folding pattern of Japanese noodles as shown in Figure 10-2. During an informal reception at MIT on August 9, 2001, Dr. Yamada told us and our students that he abstracted the idea for such a geometric rotation from looking at the way his two dogs (which were squarish in shape) looked when side-by-side.

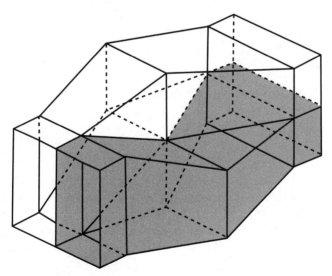

Figure 10-4. One of three segments of a concrete mixing machine

There needs to be a strong emotional tie between the CEO and real change leader—not a relationship of boss and subordinate but, rather, a partnership—a human tie. When all of the people in the Maeda company were against Dr. Maeda's desire to build a concrete mixer based on his insight about folding Japanese noodles, people were against Dr. Yamada, too. They called him a sycophant and a courtier. In reality, Dr. Yamada was a strong partner with Dr. Maeda, and Maeda would not have succeeded without Yamada.

Real change leaders, per Katzenbach, function as unique linch-pins who make connections among:

▶ Top leadership aspirations (what are we trying to become?)

▶ Workforce energy and productivity (how will we climb the mountain?)

▶ Marketplace reality (what will our target customers and potential competitors do?)

The four case studies of the previous two chapters all involve real change leaders, even though we didn't emphasize it before. They are listed in Table 10-6.

10.2 NIMS and Principles 7 and 8

Principle 7. Create an *innovative* system to provide *feedback from results*.

Principle 8. Create a daily operation system including the new *work structure*, new approach to *human capabilities*, and *improvement activities*.

Although the case of the NIMS division of NEC took place in the 1980s in Japan, we include it here because it is another excellent example of organizational transformation.[2] The story came from Kiyoshi Uchimaru who we were privileged to talk with at length on several occasions. With his colleagues, Mr. Uchimaru wrote the book [Uchimaru93] describing the efforts of NEC Integrated Circuit and Microcomputer Systems (NIMS) to implement TQM.[3] Here then is the story of NIMS.[4]

When we first came in touch with NIMS, it was a 1,000-person design subsidiary of NEC. It had started as a contract engineering shop. In time, it seemed critical for NIMS to develop self-sufficiency to manage the development of its products. Seeking to refine its methods, NIMS embarked on implementing TQM and eventually won the 1987 Deming Prize. The leader of NIMS was Kiyoshi Uchimaru, an experienced engineering manager who spent an exceptional amount of time himself on TQM diagnosis.

There are different ways to look at the NIMS story. It can be seen as a story of incrementally developing a business improvement system. (See Shiba93 and Uchimaru93 for more on this story.) Here we emphasize NIMS as a story of the systematic development of personal skill.

Engineers everywhere say things like, "Formal improvement methods might be applicable to manufacturing, but it cannot be applied to a creative task such as engineering." It was the same at NIMS. However, Uchimaru believed scientific improvement such as Deming's PDCA cycle could be applied in engineering to "pick an important problem, get the facts, analyze the facts, find the underlying truth, plan a method of improvement based on the underlying truth, systematically test it to verify that it works, standardize the new method, and then cycle around again."[5]

Not knowing exactly where to begin, Uchimaru decided to focus on two goals: first, to make the development process at NIMS more visible; second, to find mistakes earlier in the development process—to "insert quality" earlier. These issues are represented by the horizontal and vertical axes of Figure 10-5.[6]

NIMS started at the lower left corner of the figure with mistakes being found late in the process (downstream) and not much visibility into their development process. The company started its improvement process by beginning to implement TQM (TQC in the figure), and fairly soon they tried to use one of TQM's most powerful and sophisticated techniques of company-wide alignment called hoshin management. However, they were not experienced enough to make good use of hoshin management, and so they returned to the relatively fundamental improvement idea of developing some metrics by which to measure their development process.

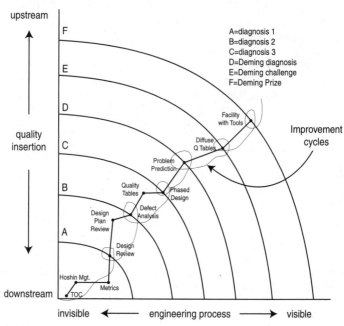

Figure 10-5. *Stages in TQM implementation at NIMS*

Notice in the figure that adding metrics makes the process a little more visible but doesn't do much to find the mistakes earlier. On the other hand, the next improvement effort was to add engineering design reviews. This clearly works on finding mistakes (e.g., in a product design) earlier. Each cycle of improvement shown in the figure improved things along one axis or the other, or both. For instance, reviewing the design plan before the design is started finds mistakes in the overall plan at an earlier time.

Next NIMS implemented a technique called defect analysis in which defects that were found were deeply analyzed to find and remove the root cause that allowed the defect to be created.

Then NIMS moved to trying to improve its designs in terms of customer acceptance, and for this they used a tool known as quality tables—large charts showing the elements of user requirements vs. metrics for measuring whether the desired elements are being delivered. These charts were so massive that they were not really useful, so NIMS settled for making long lists of the user requirements for which off-the-shelf solutions were possible and small quality tables for understanding how to implement those aspects of user requirements that necessitated innovations.

Eventually, NIMS concluded that its design process itself was not very visible, and they embarked on processes they called phased hierarchical design. They divided the development process into several-week to multi-month phases. Then, each phase was divided (at natural development steps) into shorter subphases. Having many subphases gave visibility into the process at many more points and allowed mistakes to be found earlier (e.g., after a subphase rather than at the end of a multi-month phase).

Next, Uchimaru set out to improve the professionalism (skill) of his engineers, so they would make less mistakes that needed to be found. Uchimaru said that any professional (at golf, the game of go, or VLSI design) has three characteristics [Uchimaru93]:

▶ A strong grounding in theory and the ability to apply the theory practically

▶ A large set of tools he or she knows how to use in different situations, acquired through experience (many turns of the improvement cycle mentioned above)

▶ A strong capability for analyzing failure (the professional understands why he or she made a mistake and learns from it)

Historically, professionals have always been developed through study with a master. So NIMS embarked on a process called problem prediction wherein engineering managers (themselves presumably master engineers) worked with younger engineers to better understand their designs-in-progress and to be able to see and remove design mistakes before implementation (like a chess player looks ahead from potential moves to see what problems might result). The subphases mentioned earlier were divided into still smaller (few-day) steps, and the master engineers talked with the younger engineers at the beginning and end of each smaller step to help the younger engineer learn to see and avoid potential problems. Notice that the role of the engineering manager also changed—not only the skill of the engineers.

Finally, the NIMS managers spread the techniques they had developed throughout the company.

Each of the concentric circles (labeled A, B, etc., in Figure 10-5) represents roughly a year's time, and each year included an internal or external diagnosis of the current status and what needed to be done next. Uchimaru describes these cycles of improvement and circles of diagnosis as the "spiral up of craftsmanship."

Reviewing the NIMS case study, we see parallels between the change models illustrated in Figures 9-4 and 9-7, as shown in Figure 10-6. Uchimaru's philosophy was to apply the continuous improvement techniques of the plan-do-check-act cycle and the 7 Steps for reactive improvement[7] in research and development. Uchimaru was motivated by a crisis—his business was unable to compete even though his customer was other parts of NEC. His mental breakthrough was to focus on making the process visible and looking for defects early. He revolutionized the new-design process by breaking the design process into much shorter time periods than is considered normal (another way of looking at finding defects early). Feedback came from metrics they monitored, design reviews, design plan reviews, and defect analysis.

The organizational changes were implemented using traditional Total Quality Control (or Total Quality Management) methods, particularly hoshin management.[8] In the end, successful change of the organization depended on developing a sensibility of problem identification in the NIMS engineers.

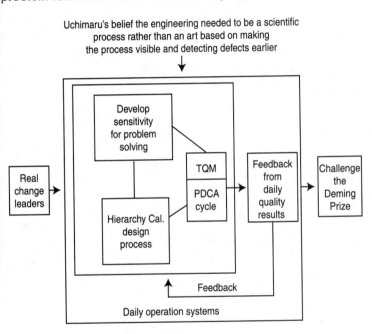

Figure 10-6. *Model for organizational change at* NIMS

10.3 Summary model

Summarizing the management models shown in Figures 9-4, 9-7, and 10-6, we derive the more-abstract model shown in Figure 10-7.[9] In the new-business-operation box, we see a typical daily operation system producing results, and the results being fed back to modify the daily operation system. Within the daily operation system are the systems that produce the work, the activities to develop the people to better do the work, and the activities aimed at getting better at doing improvement work. The new business operation is influenced by the philosophy of societal values the visionary leader has developed and espouses, and it has a target to aim for in terms of the visible image of the goal. However, such intangible forces are insufficient to ensure change. There also must be physical, organizational, and behavioral systems that constrain and channel the new business evolution and someone (the real change leader or leaders) who drives the change forward. In each of the six cases reviewed in these chapters, mechanisms were put in place to encourage changes in behavior consistent with the desired direction of transformation.

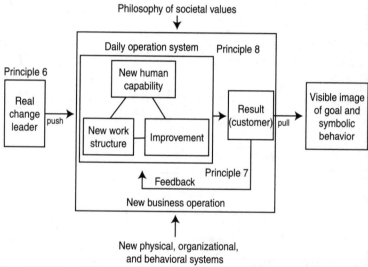

Figure 10-7. Build new business

Encouraging the change has a complication. We want the change to happen and, thus, "force the change" might be a better phrase than "encourage the change" in behavior. However, breakthrough is a process of creation. Applying the forces around the new-business-operation box in some sort of programmatic or enforced way might seem artificial and might kill the possibilities for creativity. Rather, in at least some cases, the four forces might need to be practiced more or less implicitly and subtly integrated in the movement toward the desired breakthrough. For instance, the goal should not be an explicit operational target; rather, it is a guide to the behavior of people. Top-down orders and instructions from the CEO are unlikely to enhance creativity; the leader is better off modeling the desired behavior and showing his or her personal and business character that is appropriate to making the change. Real change leaders are a way of accelerating, not necessarily enforcing, change and provide another sort of role model for the organization. The common language that is a part of a new behavioral system is not a set of declared standards; rather, it helps create an environment for acceptance of movement in the desired direction.

Breakthrough is achieved by engaging the energies and emotions of the employees, although it takes work and time to overcome their resistance to change. Trying to force or manipulate the employees to move in the desired direction will likely backfire. In 2001, Shoji Shiba visited Hewlett-Packard headquarters where he heard a senior executive say:

> We do not expect that you will work your whole life at HP. (Of course, if you stay at HP for life it will be wonderful.)...If you have a strong passion to fulfill what HP is going to do, you can utilize HP as a place to realize your dream.

The elements shown in the figure are the means to create a "dream team" capable of achieving the desired breakthrough by creating a new relationship among the people within the organization.

Figure 10-8 shows the elements of Figure 10-7 embedded in the overall context of applying the eight principles of visionary leadership.

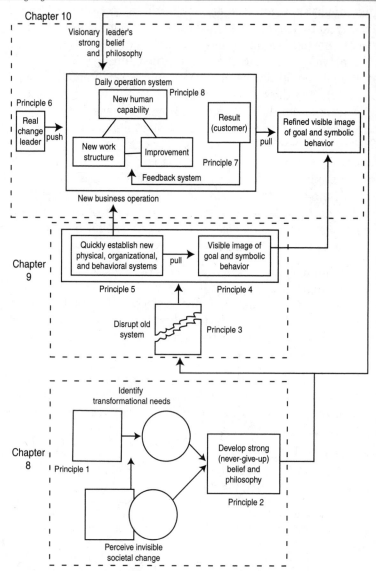

Figure 10-8. Visionary leader's path of transformation

10.4 Charts for all companies and all principles

Tables 10-1 through 10-6 on the following pages note the application of the eight principles of visionary leadership in the six case studies we have presented in detail in this and the previous two chapters. We encourage you to reread the case studies as you study these tables. Obviously, some actions in a case study address more than one principle, and in some cases the CEO might not have much used one or two of the principles.

Notes

1. The text in this section was derived from Maeda02 and Shiba01.

2. Also, this rich case study provides excellent examples of several other dimensions of business improvement useful to companies everywhere today (in the year 2005).

3. This is an unusual and important book that should be read by anyone thinking seriously about how to improve the management of a company, particularly someone trying to improve the performance of a new product development organization. Mr. Uchimaru died in the mid-1990s, a profound loss to modern management thought.

4. We also described the NIMS case study previously in Shiba93 and Shiba01; they, in turn, were derived from Uchimaru93.

5. Shiba01.

6. Which we first derived in 1991 and have included in many publications since.

7. Shiba01, Chapter 6.

8. Shiba01, Chapter 24.

9. We did not create a parallel figure for the Maeda Corporation because in that description we did not focus on the company's operational management system.

Table 10-1. Examples of Principle 1

	Value change	Outside view	On-site observation
Humanitas	From medical code to human happiness	Becker was headhunted from outside Humanitas	Becker had a gut understanding of the "misery island" state of eldercare
ZIN	From mercy forgotten to rediscovery of mercy	Brother Wim had a strong historical perspective, had gone to university, and knew the attractions outside the order	Brother Wim was deeply involved for decades in the affairs and problems of the order
FAVI	From control because man-is-bad and to trust that man-is-good	Zobrist had not developed FAVI's management system and was dropped in by helicopter to replace the retiring insider CEO	Zobrist spent four months observing before taking over as CEO
SOL	From traditional work style to freedom style	Joronen was against the family's traditional management approach	Joronen had observed the business closely daily from childhood
Maeda	Dr. Maeda became aware of the problem of mixing high performance concrete in cold regions such as Hokkaido province	Dr. Maeda was a liberal arts graduate, not an engineer; he was an outsider in the world of concrete engineering	Dr. Maeda grew up around the family-owned Maeda company and had worked extensively with the company; thus, he knew the company very well
NIMS	From engineering as art to engineering as a visible, scientific process	Uchimaru was appointed CEO of NIMS from elsewhere in NEC and with a manufacturing rather than engineering operating background	Uchimaru saw the daily defects and delays of products and services

Table 10-2. *Examples of Principle 2*

	Strong commitment	Outside-in communications
Humanitas	Becker persevered in the face of strong resistance from medical professions and restaurant losses	Becker gave journalists stories of his organization's problems, and regularly appeared on TV
ZIN	Brother Wim had long served in the senior position in the order and could have retired; instead he started the new mercy activity	Brother Wim advertised in newspapers and on TV to recruit new brothers; this was a revolutionary event and conveyed a strong message back to the organization
FAVI	Zobrist said FAVI is like a tree; we will stay in Hallencourt	Zobrist frequently appeared in the mass media and at public presentations
SOL	Joronen started SOL on her own initiative	Joronen frequently gave public presentations and appeared in the mass media
Maeda	Dr. Maeda continued in the face of broad internal criticism about the "president's folly" and at least three or four failures to develop a noodle-method-based concrete mixer	With the aid of an outside advisor, Dr. Maeda was invited to present his innovative idea for concrete mixing to an international conference in the concrete field and this, in turn, resulted in an invitation to another conference; this external validation for Dr. Maeda had strong impact on people back within the corporation and also energized Maeda himself
NIMS	Uchimaru put NIMS through years of PDCA cycles despite resistance from engineers and severe comments from outside counselors	NIMS challenging the Deming prize brought outside critiques and counselors

Table 10-3. Examples of Principle 3

	Symbolic disruptions
Humanitas	Stopped hiring consultants; let 2 of 10 healthcare professionals leave; destroyed the old style building; no white clothes for health care people; disclosed all business results; customer called "client" instead of "patient"
ZIN	Combined old church with a modern building in a prize-winning architecture combination; hired a layman to direct the new business who, in turn, used outside consultants—a big break with the traditional way of management in a closed religious order
FAVI	Abolished attendance system; stopped paying production premiums; disclosed all business results; bricked up CEO's office window
SOL	Created SOL City as a showcase, no fixed desks for people in main office, office open 24x365, CEO has no office, no secretary, and no company car
Maeda	Dr. Maeda acted in a way not typical of a Japanese CEO's behavior by continuing when almost all his engineers thought his efforts were folly
NIMS	Traditional engineering approach based on gut feel was abolished

Table 10-4. *Examples of Principle 4*

	Visible image	Leader's symbolic behavior
Humanitas	Mixed use building with its colorfully painted walls and ceilings and many activities typical of a village main street	Dr. Becker always speaks in terms of surprising, sometimes shocking, examples to illustrate the importance of client happiness in addition to health care, e.g., "five cats in a room," "a beer a day keeps the doctor away," etc.
ZIN	Church with painting of "Seven Works of Mercy" and cemetery of the brothers indicated a focus on the spiritual	Brother Wim personally lived in a traditional religious community residential situation 30–40 meters from the modern building and church, thus demonstrating a continuing spiritual commitment to the vocation of mercy as opposed to a commercial intent
FAVI	Tree-money-love illustration	CEO Zobrist blocked up the top-floor window from which he could observe the whole factory
SOL	SOL City	CEO Joronen has no executive perks, not even an office, and she always wears yellow
Maeda	Dr. Maeda made international presentations that focused attention on his innovative mixer development efforts	Dr. Maeda, a busy CEO, dedicated much of his own time to the innovative mixer project
NIMS	Challenge of Deming Prize	Mr. Uchimaru spent large amounts of time doing Hoshin diagnosis in order to diffuse TQM practices

Table 10-5. Examples of Principle 5

	Physical	Organizational	Behavioral
Humanitas	Build several new, mixed use buildings	From care to housing; extended family	Yes culture; use it or lose it philosophy
ZIN	The new building provided components of environmental context consistent with the new mission of mercy applied to a conference center setting	Creation of an organization including both laypeople and brothers	Practicing the "new mercy"
FAVI	Unlocked storage room, removal of time clocks, clean and painted factory, and physically separate mini-factories within same building	Seamless organization from customers to R&D to production to post-delivery service	Elimination of unneeded meetings in favor of worker empowerment, goal of intimate relations with customers
SOL	SOL City office layout	Establishment of self-directed work teams	Great personal freedom for employees
Maeda	The prototype machines themselves were a physical manifestation	Gradually expanding group of collaborators from Dr. Yamada to project team to joint work with outside entities; also the Maeda school established	The new breakthrough spirit and behavior is taught by the Maeda school
NIMS	Many parts of the new development process have physical manifestations	TQM infrastructure organization set up	Basing actions on facts derived using TQM methods

Table 10-6. *Examples of Principles 6, 7, and 8*

	P6: Real change leaders	P7: Feedback system	P8: Daily operations system
Humanitas	Managers of the individual apartment complexes and some head office managers who provide strong support to Dr. Becker	Moments of truth with clients	Flat organization with outside volunteers
ZIN	Director of the ZIN business	Moments of truth with seminar participants	Involvement of outside experts with the dedicated brothers
FAVI	Chiefs of the mini-factories, the commercial person who interfaces among the customers, mini-factories and R&D, and the R&D leaders	Direct, close relationships among customers, mini-factories, and R&D; the commercial person is key to making this feedback system work	Integrated R&D and mini-factories, constantly exploring outside information
SOL	Leaders of the self-directed work teams and the head office managers	Five types of customer feedback	Self-directed work teams with intensive skill training
Maeda	Dr. Yamada	Testing of the prototype concrete mixers in real business situations	M-Y Mixer is in daily use in Maeda's business and the Maeda school to develop a new generation of employees with a breakthrough mentality
NIMS	TQM facilitators and some line managers who strongly supported Mr. Uchimaru and developed the hierarchical design methods	PDCA cycle in daily work, Hoshin planning and review process, and TQM system diagnosis by the Deming committee	Explicit engineering design and development process, TQM practices, and problem sensing practices

Bibliography

Ackoff81 Ackoff, Russell L. *Creating the Corporate Future: Plan or Be Planned For.* Wiley, 1981.

Bhalla97 *Quotes of Gandhi* (compiled by Shalu Bhalla), New Delhi: UBS Publishers' Distribution Ltd., 1997.

Bower97 Bower, Joseph L. Harvard Business School Case: "Teradyne: The Aurora Project" (revised March 29, 1999). Boston: Harvard Business School Press, 1997.

Bower98 Bower, Joseph L. Harvard Business School Case: "Teradyne: Corporate Management of Disruptive Change" (revised March 25, 1999). Boston: Harvard Business School Press, 1998.

Burt04 Burt, Ronald S. "Structural Holes and Good Ideas." *American Journal of Sociology* 110 (2005): 349-399.

Challapalli00 Challapalli, Sally, Michael Chu, Annie Kuo, Emily Liu, Arundhati Singh, and Erick Tseng. "Teradyne's Aurora Project." MIT class 6.933 (2000), http://web.mit.edu/6.933/www/final1.pdf.

Christensen97 Christensen, Clayton. *The Innovator's Dilemma: When New Technologies Cause Great Firms to Fail.* Boston: Harvard Business School Press, 1997. Professor Christensen has written later books and papers elaborating on his ideas relating to the innovator's dilemma.

Derveux98 Derveux, Isabelle. "Manet, Monet, and The Gare Saint-Lazare," exhibition brochure. Washington, D.C.: National Gallery of Art, 1998. http://www.nga.gov/feature/manet/manetbro.pdf

Drucker93 Drucker, Peter. *Innovation and Entrepreneurship*, paperback edition. Collins, 1993.

Foster86 Foster, Richard. *Innovation: The Attacker's Advantage.* New York: Summit Books, 1986.

Gates96 Gates, Bill, Nathan Myhrvold, and Peter M. Rinearson. *The Road Ahead*, paperback edition. Penguin USA, 1996.

Gates99 Gates, Bill, and Collins Hemingway. *Business @ the Speed of Thought.* New York: Warner Books, 1999.

Gerstner03 Gerstner, Louis. *Who Says Elephants Can't Dance?*, paperback edition. HarperBusiness, 2003.

Griffin91 Griffin, Abbie, and John Hauser, "The Voice of the Customer." Working Paper 92-2, MIT Marketing Center, Cambridge, MA, January 1991.

Grove99 Grove, Andrew S. *Only the Paranoid Survive: How to Exploit the Crisis Points That Challenge Every Company*, paperback edition. Currency, 1999.

Hayakawa90 Hayakawa, S.I., and Alan R. Hayakawa. *Language in Thought and Action*, fifth edition. Harcourt, Inc., 1990.

Johnson98 Johnson, Spencer. *Who Moved My Cheese? An Amazing Way to Deal with Change in Your Work and in Your Life.* Putnam Adult, 1998.

Katzenbach95 Katzenbach, Jon R. *Real Change Leaders*, Random House, 1995.

Kobayashi86 Kobayashi, Koji. *Computers and Communications: A Vision of C&C.* Cambridge, MA: MIT Press, 1986.

Kobayashi91 Kobayashi, Koji. *The Rise of NEC: How the World's Greatest Company Is Managed.* Cambridge, MA: Blackwell Publishers, 1991.

Lefebvre06 Lefebvre, Jean, and Shoji Shiba. "Collaboration and Trust in the Supply Chain: The Case of FAVI S.A.", to be published. *Supply Chain Forum: an International Journal*, Special Issue on Collaboration and Trust in the Supply Chain (2006).

Liker04 Liker, Jeffery K. *The Toyota Way.* McGraw-Hill, 2004.

Lillrank89 Lillrank, Paul, and Noriaki Kano. *Continuous Improvement: Quality Control Circles in Japanese Industry.* Ann Arbor: Center for Japanese Studies, The University of Michigan, 1989.

Maeda02 Maeda, Matabee Kenji. "Creativity from Adversity—Three Breakthroughs at Maeda Corporation." *Center for Quality of Management Journal* 10.2 (Winter 2001): 3–17.

Marrewijk04 Marrewijk, Marcel, and Hans Becker. "The Hidden Hand of Cultural Governance: The Transformation Process of Humanitas, a Community-Driven Organization Providing Cure, Care, Housing and Well-being to Elderly People." *Journal of Business Ethics* 55.2 (December 2004): 205–214.

Meyers05 Meyers, Jeffrey. *Impressionist Quartet: The Intimate Genius of Manet and Morisot, Degas and Cassatt*. Orlando, FL: Harcourt, Inc., 2005.

Nonaka95 Nonaka, Ikujiro, and Hirotaka Takeuchi. *The Knowledge-Creating Company: How Japanese Companies Create the Dynamics of Innovation*. Oxford University Press, USA, 1995.

O'Reilly04 O'Reilly, Charles A. III, and Michael L. Tushman. "The Ambidextrous Organization." *Harvard Business Review* 82.4 (April 2004): 77–81.

Shiba93 Shiba, Shoji, Alan Graham, and David Walden. *A New American TQM: Four Practical Revolutions in Management*. New York: Productivity Press, 1993.

Shiba98 Shiba, Shoji (English transcription by David Walden). "Leadership and Breakthrough." *Center for Quality of Management Journal* 7.2 (Winter 1998): 10–22.

Shiba01 Shiba, Shoji, and David Walden. *Four Practical Revolutions in Management: Systems for Creating Unique Organizational Quality*. New York: Productivity Press, 2001.

Shiba03 Shiba, Shoji. *Breakthrough Management* (in Japanese). 1-2-1, Motdishi - Nihonbashi Chuo-Ku, Tokyo Japan - 103-8345: Toyo Keizai Publishing Company, 2003.

Shiba05 Shiba, Shoji. *The Five Step Discovery Process Manual*, document 01-2005. Gurgaon, Haryana, India, fax (0124) 5014051 : Confederation of Indian Industry, February 2005.

Spear99 Spear, Steven, and H. Kent Bowen. "Decoding the DNA of the Toyota Production System." *Harvard Business Review* (September-October 1999): 97–106.

Spear04 Spear, Steven J. "Learning to Lead at Toyota." *Harvard Business Review* (May 2004): 78–86.

Tushman02 Tushman, Michael L., and Charles A. O'Reilly III. *Winning Through Innovation*. Boston: Harvard Business School Press, 2002.

Uchimaru93 Uchimaru, Kiyoshi, Susumu Okamoto, Bunteru Kurahara, and Keisuke Arai (forward by David Walden). *TQM for Technical Groups: Total Quality Principles for Product Development*. New York: Productivity Press, 1993.

Walden93   Walden, David. "Breakthrough and Continuous Improvement in Research and Development—An Essay." *Center for Quality of Management Journal* 2.2 (Spring 1993): 25–29.

Webb66   Webb, Eugene J., Donald T. Campbell, Richard D. Schwartz, and Lee Sechrest. *Unobtrusive Measures, Non-Reactive Research in the Social Sciences.* Chicago: Rand McNally & Company, 1966. A second, revised edition was published by SAGE Publications in 1999.

Wilson98   Wilson-Bareau, Juliet. *Manet, Monet, and the Gare Saint-Lazare.* Washington and New Haven: National Gallery of Art Washington and Yale University Press, 1998.